American

Theocracy

Unpacked:

Arguments Disassembled, Implications Examined, And A Way Forward Suggested

W. Frederick Zimmerman

NIMBLE BOOKS LLC

NIMBLE BOOKS LLC

ISBN: 0-9777424-9-0

Copyright 2006 W. Frederick Zimmerman

Last saved 2007-09-14.

Nimble Books, LLC

2006 Medford Suite C127

Ann Arbor, MI 48104-4963

http://www.nimblebooks.com

Contents

Book description

When I began reading *American Theocracy,* the best-seller by Kevin Phillips, I felt almost immediately that this was an excellent and thought-provoking book that was so wrong about so many fundamental issues that it demanded a strong, immediate, and highly focused response.

This book, American *Theocracy Unpacked,* takes advantage of electronic publishing technology to provide that "nimble" response, less than three months after I started reading Phillips's book. I take a close, almost paragraph-by-paragraph look at Phillips's arguments. I am confident that the result is respectful but stimulating. I acknowledge and applaud his many important insights, but I also suggest a way forward that is less fearful of an "American theocracy," and, indeed, more hopeful for America and the world.

In the body of the book, I have used the informal, rather "bulletized" house style that Nimble Books has used to produce "living books" on subjects ranging from Harry Potter and Dan Brown to science, politics, technology, and medicine.

NIMBLE BOOKS LLC

Publisher's Comments

U.S. AND INTERNATIONAL RIGHTS

U.S. and international republication rights are available for this title; to discuss, please send e-mail to rights@nimblebooks.com.

ABOUT NIMBLE BOOKS

Our trusty Merriam-Webster Collegiate Dictionary defines "nimble" as follows:

> 1: quick and light in motion: AGILE *nimble fingers*
>
> 2 a: marked by quick, alert, clever conception, comprehension, or resourcefulness *a nimble mind* b: RESPONSIVE, SENSITIVE *a nimble listener*

And traces the etymology to the 14th Century:

> Middle English nimel, from Old English numol holding much, from niman to take; akin to Old High German neman to take, Greek nemein to distribute, manage, nomos pasture, nomos usage, custom, law

The etymology is reminiscent of the old Biblical adage, "to whom much is given, much is expected" (Luke 12:48). Nimble Books seeks to honor that Christian principle by combining the spirit of *nimbleness* with the Biblical concept of *abundance:* we deliver what you need to know about a subject in a quick, resourceful, and sensitive manner.

vi

Author's comments

READ THIS BOOK IF ...

- You thought *American Theocracy* was an important book.

- You are interested in a far-ranging, open-minded meditation on the issues Phillips raises.

- You are a Christian who is wondering how to be "salt and light" in a world that fears theocracy.

DON'T BOTHER IF ...

- You are expecting me to disagree with everything in *American Theocracy*.

- You are expecting me to attack Kevin Phillips as a person.

- You aren't willing to read *American Theocracy*.

NIMBLE BOOKS LLC

Author bio

W. Frederick Zimmerman is an attorney, technologist, and publisher who lives in Ann Arbor, Michigan. He is the author of dozens of books and technical papers on topics ranging from Harry Potter to global climate change.

Acknowledgements

Cheryl, Kelsey, and Parker, as always.

Kevin Phillips, for writing a provocative, thoughtful, and entertaining book.

NIMBLE BOOKS LLC

How this book is organized and what it contains

This book follows the same structure as *American Theocracy*, with the addition of some introductory and interstitial comments.   It is recommended that you have a copy of *American Theocracy* on hand as you read.

Dedication

SMART-ALEC SUMMARY: "To everyone who agrees with me."

SLIGHTLY MORE FAIR-MINDED SUMMARY: The dedication is to the "millions" of Republicans disenchanted with the results of the 2000 and 2004 elections and the "disenlightenment" they produced. These are telling words.

JUST HOW MANY MILLIONS IS "MILLIONS?" This is not the place to attempt the calculation, but one could make a stab at it using survey research, or, better yet, the results of the 2006 election. My gut feeling is that it is not that many millions compared with the number of millions of Republicans who got what they expected when they voted for George W. and who are not planning to change their party allegiance next time around.

In other words, this book is dedicated to a minority. Why didn't Phillips broaden the scope of the dedication a bit and include the many more millions of Democrats who are even more disenchanted? The straightforward answer is that Phillips still feels some party loyalty. The slightly more subtle answer is that he thinks Democrats don't need this book, because they already know what to do.

I HAVE TO WONDER WHETHER IT IS HELPFUL to start flinging around the word "disenlightenment" within the first 50 words of a book. You might as well just call those who voted against you "ignorant boobs" and be done with it.

THE OPPOSITE OF "DISENLIGHTENMENT" is, of course, the Enlightenment, the intellectual movement commonly associated with the 18th Century opening of the European mind. I myself am a great fan of Enlightenment values, but it is hard to be excited about rallying round a movement that saw its glory days three hundred years ago. The rallying cry can't be "Back to the Enlightenment!" -- and that means that we can't just leave the indictment as "disenlightenment."

Preface

SMART-ALEC SUMMARY: Things have gone to hell in a hand-basket since I wrote my first book.

QUESTIONABLE ASSUMPTIONS GALORE enhance this spritely preface, beginning with the very first sentence: "The American people are not fools." Oh, really? Didn't P. T. Barnum have something different to say about that?

(Well, no ... apparently Barnum is often falsely credited with saying there's a sucker born every minute. According to the vastly authoritative Wikipedia,

> "the source of the quote is most likely famous con-man Joseph ("Paper Collar" Joe) Bessimer. Barnum's fellow circus owner and arch-rival Adam Forepaugh attributed the quote to Barnum in a newspaper interview in an attempt to discredit him."[1])

Leaving P. T. Barnum out of it, I suspect that most of us would agree that there *is* a sucker born every minute! Thousands of years of what the modern age calls "wisdom literature" and "political theory" suggests that well, yes, people are mostly fools, both considered as individuals and in the aggregate. And there is a very substantial body of people, both in the United States and outside it, who believe that Americans, are, if anything, more foolish than ordinary people. At a minimum, it is Cavalier for Phillips to vault

---

[1] http://en.wikipedia.org/wiki/There_is_a_sucker_born_every_minute

3

to the cheerful conclusion that the American people know what they're doing when (selected polls) have ("so often") said we are on the "wrong track."

Oh, and the argument that we're on the "wrong track" is based on *polls!* It must be true, then.

In short, it is scarcely confidence-inspiring that Phillips starts off with such a tremendous bout of hand-waving.

THE THREE PERILS to the American future that he identifies – oil dependency, radicalized religion, and debt – seem reasonable to me, but they are not quite up to the Four Horsemen standard of War, Famine, Pestilence, and Death.   There's a reason why broad fears tend to have staying power: overspecialized fears tend to miss the unexpected. Phillips is perfectly correct in saying that war and terror "derive much of their current impetus" from what I would describe as the fortuitous location of huge oil reserves underneath the holy lands of Islam, but he may well be suffering from a poverty of futuristic imagination when he assumes that oil and Islam will continue to be the major causes of war and terror throughout the 21st Century. If modern history shows us anything, it is that we don't know what the hell to expect next (or, as Henry Ford put it, "history is one damn thing after another.")

WHEE! MORAL EQUIVALENCE! And you thought that went out of style at the end of the Cold War. No, Kevin Phillips is still here to fight the good fight by equating the excesses of American and Israeli fundamentalism with the harm done by radical Islam. Gee, there's at least one major difference, which is that even the most outrageous American fundamentalists (and I hold no affection for Jerry Falwell or Pat Robertson) don't provide the moral and practical leadership and funding for **suicide murders.**

PHILLIPS IS RIGHT ON TARGET, as far as I'm concerned, when he writes about the pernicious emergence of the "debt-and-credit industrial complex." I am a bit more skeptical when he **blames it all on the Bush family,** but I haven't read *American Dynasty* yet.

THINLY VEILED SUBTEXT: "Read my previous bestseller."

Is the "southern-dominated, biblically-driven Washington GOP" **a rogue coalition?** That's an interesting phrase, but what exactly does it mean to say that a coalition is a "rogue"? Merriam-Webster OnLine defines rogue (adj.) as follows:

> **1** *of an animal* : being vicious and destructive
>
> **2** : resembling or suggesting a rogue elephant especially in being isolated and dangerous or uncontrollable <capsized by a *rogue* wave>

Isn't the whole point of coalitions in a democracy to help people get what they want? Talking about a "rogue coalition" is like talking about a "rogue majority" – it's a colorful phrase that suggests foul play and danger, but those qualities are, of course, strictly in the eye of the beholder.

MORE THINLY VEILED SUBTEXT: "I, Kevin Phillips, invented the phrase 'Sun Belt,' so this whole mess is basically my fault."

WILLIAM SAFIRE AND KEVIN PHILLIPS liked the writings of Sir Halford Mackinder, who thought control of the Eurasian "heartland" would determine control of the world, but it's not clear why, since **Mackinder was obviously wrong.** Victory in World War One went to the peripheral European powers of France and Great Britain, and to the Oceanic powers of the United States and Japan. The oceanic Allies purchased their victory in World War Two at a far more affordable price than the Soviet Union, which had to spend 20 million lives to regain control of the Eurasian heartland, a territory which availed the former Soviet Union precisely nothing at the end of the Cold War.

When Phillips brings the analogy closer to home, talking about the heartland of America, I am reminded that the Union won the Civil

War by controlling Virginia, the seas, and the Mississippi: not Kansas.

Phillips tries to save Mackinder's thesis by talking about the "Eurasian cockpit," as the "pivot of the international struggle for oil", but c'mon, who are we kidding? The Islamic countries have most of the world's oil, and they still feel oppressed and overwhelmed, at the mercy of Western and Israeli "boots on the ground." If controlling the heartland is so great, why isn't it the ticket to victory for the people who live there?

A BIT MORE ABOUT MACKINDER for those who are curious. This hand-drawn image from his *Democratic Ideals and Reality: A Study in the Politics of Reconstruction* via **the heroes at Google Book Search**[2] actually gives a pretty good insight into his thinking about the Heartland.

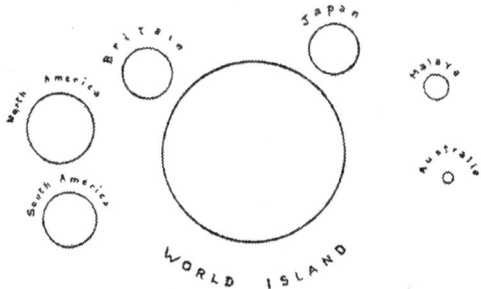

FIG. 13.—These circles represent the relative populations of the World-Island and its satellites.

Figure 1. Mackinder's World Island and its satellites

---

[2]   http://googleblog.blogspot.com/2006/02/defending-future-of-books.html

The Heartland is all the stuff on the inside of the World Island that is inaccessible to sea-faring peoples and therefore is a possible sanctuary for a continental power that might rival Great Britain, or, now, the United States. In the American context, the Heartland is **the stuff in the "flyover zone" that is impervious to liberal messaging.**

PHILLIPS DESCRIBES OHIO, along with Wyoming and Colorado, as "the seat of a fossil-fuels political alliance," which is sloppy thinking, since Ohio almost went Democratic in 2004 and its large cities are full of liberals. There is quite a difference between Ohio and Wyoming.

PHILLIPS SEEMS TO ENVY CAESAR AND NAPOLEON and their willingness to use force, but suggests that modern American Presidents are more hamstrung by economic risks than those two tyrants were. In fact, the British embargo of the Continent and the economic-demographic disaster caused by Napoleon's war had a great deal to do with the Emperor's downfall.

WHEE! MORE SWEEPING GENERALIZATIONS! Phillips pulls no punches in describing "evangelicals, fundamentalists, and Pentacostals" as credulous believes in an imminent "end times" Armageddon.

WHY PEOPLE WHO AREN'T RELIGIOUS LOVE TO WRITE ABOUT RELIGION is **a puzzler** to me. Phillips presents himself as someone who has read and thought about religion for years, culminating in his 1998 Pulitzer-nominated *The Cousin's Wars*. Why, Phillips observes, he and his wife even love to tour historical churches!

I must be fair: it is wrong of me to assume that Phillips and his wife are not religious. But what I can observe with justice is that in this preface, Phillips spends quite a bit of time writing about religion as observed from the exterior, and absolutely no time writing about it as observed from the interior—which means that he winds up with very little common ground with the tens or hundreds of millions of Americans who base their lives on the Bible. That's a shame.

THE GOLDILOCKS FALLACY appears here in Phillips's potted history of religion in America: there was, apparently, too much religion in the United States before the 1960s, when "secular advocates" made **the huge honking mistake** of trying to "push Christianity out of the public square," which, as Phillips observes, seems to have **backfired big-time** by prodding outraged religious groups to take a more active role in the public arena. First too much, then too little, now too much again! Exactly what does Phillips think religion's role should be in the public arena?

THE "T" BOMB makes its first appearance as Phillips refers to "strong theocratic pressures" on the Republican national coalition. The use of the word "pressures" is a telling qualification, as it subtly distances Phillips from actually defining our current form of government as a theocracy.

THEOCRACY (N.) ACCORDING TO THE ONLINE FREE DICTIONARY:

A government ruled by or subject to religious authority.

A state so governed.

THEOCRACY (N.) ACCORDING TO THE OPEN SOURCE WIKTIONARY:

Government under the control of a Church or state-sponsored religion.

1. Rule by God.[3]

---

[3] http://en.wiktionary.org/wiki/theocracy

WHEN I THINK ABOUT THEOCRACIES, I think about **hydraulic societies ruled by priest-emperors.** It is a sloppy exaggeration to say that the government of the United States is under the control of a church or a state-sponsored religion. We don't have a single national church here like the Catholic Church in pre-Revolutionary France. In fact, we have hundreds of thousands of churches, not one. Nor do we have a state-sponsored religion. In fact, we have a fundamental amendment to our Constitution that explicitly forbids establishing a state religion.

> Congress shall make no law respecting an establishment of religion, or prohibiting the free exercise thereof…

So how can we possibly have a theocracy, unless the Supreme Court is falling down on the job?

CONTEXT IS IMPORTANT. The United States has vibrant religious bodies that are actively concerned with public life. So does Iran and most of the Muslim world. But, unlike the Muslim world, the United States is also the home of the world's most vibrant, most contagious secular culture that is (to put it mildly) often organized along principles inconsistent with Christianity. It's absurd to talk about the United States as a "theocracy" when one could with equal justice talk about the United States as a "celebritocracy", a "technocracy", a "meritocracy", or a "capitalocracy." We are bigger and more diverse than that.

Is there perhaps a causal connection between America's heightened religiosity and its heightened secularity? In some sense, does fervid evangelism cause the Britney Spears phenomenon? Aimee Semple McPherson? Perhaps, perhaps … but not in the minds of most believers, or most devoutly secular people for that matter; and isn't it in some way fundamentally disrespectful to explain people's values in terms of beliefs that they themselves reject?

POLITICIZED RELIGIOSITY, in Phillips's world view, seems to be the cause of a lot of bad things ... the invasion of Iraq, clashes with science, and, worst of all, **lackluster sales of hardcover nonfiction.** Phillips seems to be rather offended that while Tim LaHaye's *Left Behind* series has sold 60 million copies, mainstream "volumes able to sell two or three hundred thousand hardcover copies" are uncommon. He cites no less a literary and scholarly authority than Jerry Falwell as "probably the most influential religious publishing event since the Bible."

DOES THE SOURCE (FALWELL) MAKE THE ASSERTION TRUE? Uh, no ... no matter what Jerry Falwell thinks, the *Left Behind* series was *not* the most influential religious publishing event since the Bible. I read the first volume, and, to be kind, **the Left Behind books are pretty poor fiction.**

IS ONE DATA POINT REPRESENTATIVE OF TWO HUNDRED FIFTY MILLION DATA POINTS? Uh, no ... just because Jerry Falwell likes *the Left Behind* books does not mean that the books are an accurate proxy for the political views of American Christians.

PHILLIPS REVERSE-ENGINEERS A FACT-FREE CONSPIRACY THEORY by noting some amazing, stunning, incredible, mind-jarring similarities (three of them!) between George W. Bush's call for war in Iraq and the *Left Behind* series. The similarities are:

the villain in Left Behind is based in Iraq;

Bush, like the heroes of Left Behind, talked about democracy and God rather than, well, oil theft as the rationale for Iraq;

Bush, like *Left Behind,* was sometimes hostile to the United Nations.

Wow, that proves it! Bush must have had a copy of Left Behind on his desk as he planned the war. Phillips offers absolutely no factual support for the theory that these books influenced the Bush administration: no interviews, no footnotes, no nothing. The best he can do is to quote Bill Moyers (could there be anyone less informed about the inner workings of the Bush administration?) to the effect that "the delusional is no longer marginal." Bill, Kevin: **the delusional has *never* been marginal in American politics,** or anywhere else. Remember the Jim Crow laws?

Instead of making up "just so stories" about the connection between popular fiction and government decision-making, it seems far more reasonable to me to rely on, say, Bob Woodward's Iraq book **based on hundreds of hours of direct interviews with decision makers** for an understanding of the Iraq war.

As far as the incredible similarities between *Left Behind* and the Iraq war:

LaHaye made a good guess in picking Iraq ... but the Euphrates is not known as the "Cradle of Civilizations" for nothing. One might as well blame Tom Clancy for 9/11 because he had a 747 crash into the Capitol in one of his novels.

Amazing! People tend to put a good face on their motivations.

The United Nations is a **poorly managed and incredibly inefficient bureaucracy** that has a wildly uneven track record of political vision and leadership. Hostility towards the UN may be unwise, but it is not delusional.

PHILLIPS THINKS WE'RE THE STUPIDEST EMPIRE IN WORLD HISTORY: "No leading world power in modern memory has become ... even a partial captive of the sort of biblical inerrancy that dismisses modern knowledge and science." Oh, really? So a belief in Biblical inerrancy is equivalent to dismissing modern knowledge and science? Try telling that to the literally billions of Christians worldwide who both believe in an inerrant Bible *and* rely on modern knowledge and science for clean water and medical treatment.

My brother Carl commented here:

> I think writing about how Christians integrate
> these topics together in their world-view and life
> would be very interesting at least for those of us
> who are less religious. Another chapter could be
> on modern media technology and religious practice.
> Liberals and non-religious people don't "GET" this
> push and pull process.

I told him that the relationship between Christianity and safe drinking water is like the relationship between the idea of evolution & medicine -- would you want to go to a doctor who didn't "believe in" evolution? Most people, including church-goers, seem to go reputable hospitals there are relatively few christians who actually modify their medical care practices to suit their doctrine -- and the ones who do (Jehovah's witnesses, Christian Science) are in my opinon crossing over the line into loonydom.

I find it possible to believe in an inerrant Bible by reminding myself that what we understand about science and the true nature of the universe is, to put it mildly, a point sample from our limited vantage point here in a wafer-thin time slice on one of 100 billion suns in an 11-dimensional string theory universe of enormous complexity. "Push pull" is a good phrase but I think there's also a sense in which we have to understand the Bible and science as simply occupying different realms. In my view, the Bible is not a biology textbook, but science can't rule out the possibility that it is an incredibly sophisticated and (sometimes) subtle communications device that operates on principles we simply will never be equipped to understand.

THE EARTH REVOLVES AROUND THE SUN, and the United States is not special, according to Phillips's version of the Copernican revolution (also known as the Principle of Mediocrity). We're just like all the other "empires", just like Earth is just like all the other planets that revolve around all the other suns. The United States, like other "empires" that have gone before it, is in the midst of a decline caused by an unholy trifecta of "religious excess, an outdated ... energy and industrial base, and financialization and debt ... from overstretch."

Except that there is one **huge honking difference** between Earth and other planets: Earth is the only planet known so far to hold life. So it is sort of special after all ... and hey, look at this: the United States is where we happen to live! So maybe it's a little bit special too...

NOT VERY THINLY VEILED AT ALL SUBTEXT: As the closing note in this Preface, Phillips promises to explore just how much the "governing Republican coalition" is to blame for the problems he has identified. **It's all about the finger-pointing!**

ADVANCING THE DEBATE: How can we change the discussion of the issues raised in American Theocracy to make the process, and the outcome, more constructive? From this analysis of the preface, it is possible to suggest a few procedural ground rules that should help.

1. Avoid sweeping generalizations.

2. Remember that context is important. Two things that are similar but are located in completely different contexts are not identical.

3. Remember that one, two, or three data points are usually not statistically significant.

4. Don't stretch words past their dictionary meanings.

5. Report specific, attributed facts to authenticate your version of events.

On the substantive side, I'd suggest the following points of departure based on this preface.

1. When we talk about geopolitics, let's not rely on Edwardian-era experts like Harland Mackinder **who tell an intriguing story that is, unfortunately, wrong.** As Phillips glancingly acknowledges at one point, there has been a whole century of thought about geopolitics since Mackinder.

2. When we talk about the future that American faces, let's remember that, as modern day sage Donald Rumsfeld so pithily articulated for a tantalized public, there are always "known unknowns "and "unknown unknowns." Oil, debt, and theocracy *may* be the three biggest problems the United States has to worry about for the next *n* years... *or* **the biggest problems may be something entirely new and unforeseen.**

3. Christians have been talking about the relationship between politics and religion for two thousand years. Is it too much to ask that commentators on "American Theocracy" be able to articulate and understand Christian perspectives on the subject?

Fuel and National Power

SMART-ALEC SUMMARY: We're running out of oil and we're screwed.

EPIGRAPHS FROM HENRY KISSINGER, SPENCER ABRAHAM, AND PAUL ROBERTS on the theme of "energy is important" fail to impress this reader. Hasn't Phillips noticed that **Kissinger has passed his sell-by date** as an expert on geopolitics? The farther away the seventies become, the more bizarre it seems that this politicking academic was ever regarded as **a rock star and wise man.** What were they smoking?

As for Spencer Abraham, who is quoted telling members of the American Petroleum Institute that they "played a large part" in making the twentieth century the "American Century", a public compliment from a Cabinet Secretary to his trade group has the analytical weight of, well, absolutely nothing. And Paul Roberts is rolled out to prove that "our brilliant energy success comes at great cost" by listing a series of things that were all a heck of a lot worse in the 70s.

I have to give Phillips credit for Roberts's interesting observation that "the industrial-strength confidence that was a by-product of our global energy economy for most of the twentieth century has slowly been replaced by anxiety." This provocative assertion cannot fail to appeal to anyone who is more than a little anxious about the future. But wait a minute ... has Roberts (and Phillips) completely forgotten about **the Internet boom** of the 90s **when America was seized with a mega-dose of industrial-strength confidence?** Instead of broadly asserting that America is becoming more and more anxious as oil becomes scarcer, it seems more accurate to me to hold the view that America's industrial "self-confidence" goes up and down in waves that are sometimes but not always driven by energy prices.

PHILLIPS BRIEFLY DISAVOWS what he calls a "vaguely Marxian mineral determinism—linking nations' power to natural resources in a way that downplays factors such as religion, nationalism, or charismatic leadership." Since that is exactly what he does in the remainder of the chapter, it is a bit odd to see him disavowing it! He spends one sentence caveating that "fuel has been one of several pivots", then the remaining thirty pages focusing strictly on just one pivot, fuel.

PHILLIPS'S THEORY OF NATIONAL POWER might be summarized as **"oil plus."** In his view, it's not just barrels in the ground that count. It's also a whole complex set of cultural adaptations and affinities that enable particular nations to be more effective at turning energy resources into power than others. Phillips deserves credit for making this subtle and important point, but it undercuts another aspect of his argument. Some of the time, Phillips is arguing that certain nations are special in their abilities to exploit resources; at other times, Phillips is arguing that America is, in the end, a declining empire like all the others, and not special at all. Which is it: **are we special or not?**

I agree with Phillips's basic thesis, that some nations do have networks of expertise that provide them with advantages that are difficult or impossible to reproduce. Oil technology was indeed one such area of American advantage in the 20th century. Where Phillips goes wrong is that he doesn't follow his argument to its logical conclusion! As a matter of fact, the United States has enjoyed a whole host of network expertise advantages in the 20th and 21st centuries, in a wide range of domains not limited to oil. To name only a few: higher education; the entertainment industries, including movies, music, and sports; and information technology. To be sure, our oil skills have helped in higher education (*see* University of Texas), movie production, but it would be wrong to attribute those positive developments solely to the oil industry (disappointing as that might be to the guys who wrote those Mobil advertorials on the Op-Ed page of *The New York Times* for so many years).

The source of these diverse yet mutually reinforcing network advantages, I would argue, is precisely America's specialness: the mixing bowl culture that combines liberty, respect for property rights, diversity, and entrepreneurial zest.

PHILLIPS RIGHTLY WORRIES ABOUT AMERICA'S AGING OIL INFRASTUCTURE, but he misses an important point when he discusses how Britain faced the crisis of 1914 to 1945 with a "sooty" aged coal infrastructure. The visionary Admiral Sir Jackie Fisher was instrumental in moving the Royal Navy from coal to oil in the years 1914. This vastly increased the RN's operational flexibility and certainly contributed to Great Britain's command of the seas from 1914 to 1945, without which national survival might have been at risk. This suggests that wise choices about strategic reliance on scarce resources can play a key role in extending national power for decades.

HYMAN RICKOVER, THE FATHER OF THE NUCLEAR NAVY, may be the equivalent of Jackie Fisher in this story. The U.S. fleet of nuclear submarines guarantees the U.S. Navy the ability to perform sea denial (if not necessarily sea control) for the foreseeable future. The nuclear example highlights that there have been significant technological options for diversifying energy resources since the 1950s. Unfortunately, **even nuclear aircraft carriers have a voracious appetite for jet fuel,** so the Rickover advantage from using next-generation energy for the modern U.S. Navy(like the Jackie Fisher advantage of switching the Royal Navy early to coal) is only a partial solution to the problem of a declining energy infrastructure.

TO THE SATISFACTION OF CONSPIRACY THEORISTS EVERYWHERE, it turns out there is an important connection between Jackie Fisher and *The Da Vinci Code.* The judge in the plagiarism suit against Dan Brown, Justice Peter Smith, included a secret code in his 71-

page judgment ... and the solution is JACKIE FISHER: WHO ARE YOU? DREADNOUGHT. *Dreadnought,* of course, was the name of the first all-big-gun battleship, developed by Fisher, and the quintessential expression of Britain's coal-era industrial might. Will future American jurists look back to Kevin Phillips for inspiration as Mr. Justice Smith looked back to Jackie Fisher? Somehow, I doubt it ... it is much more inspiring to be the symbol of an empire's reach than the herald of its overreach!

AS PHILLIPS CONCLUDES THIS INTRODUCTORY SECTION OF HIS FIRST CHAPTER, he unfortunately continues to exaggerate his case. He refers to the "trauma" of three dollar a gallon gas prices among "rural, small-town, and exurban Americans." From my reading of the news, "trauma" is too strong a word. (As George Will, not usually one of my favorite pundits, pointed out in *Newsweek*[4], the real, inflation-adjusted price of gas in April 1981 was **$3.10**). Most people seem to be making sensible adjustments in behavior: purchasing smaller cars and scaling back on discretionary driving. He rightly points out that global demand is increasing, but unwisely points to the fact that energy analysts are using scary titles in current books as a proof of coming resource wars. "War scare" books are as old as publishing. You might say the Book of Revelations is one! Although that may seem like a terribly worldly way to look at a book of the Bible, perhaps it is not a complete coincidence that God chose to end the Bible as He began it, with a bang. Surely He wants us to pay attention to the danger of evil!

THE GIST OF the next section, *A Brief History of Western Fuelishness,* is that the history of oil is important and began a long time ago. As a former history major, I can scarcely disagree. However, I think Phillips focuses on the wrong slice of the deep past. Whereas Phillips begins his history with Greek fire and tries

---

[4] *Newsweek,* May 8, 2006, at 80.

to persuade me that the history of oil from the Middle Ages to 1861 is important to the current day, I would argue that the history should begin a lot earlier—say, around two hundred fifty million years earlier!--and that the years where the current supply of oil was laid down are far more important than the years when exploitation was statistically negligible. I would have appreciated a geological excursion at this point in the book, but that's my bias towards understanding first principles and ultimate causes.

N=3 in Phillips's comparative history of leading economic powers: he identifies the Netherlands (wind and water), Great Britain (coal), and the United States (oil) as "hegemons" that have enjoyed periods of economic dominance based on superior skill at exploiting a particular energy resource. The problem is that a sample of three empires is simply not a large enough sample to justify the weight of the comparisons that Phillips makes.

AGAIN, CONTEXT IS IMPORTANT: the nation-state system in 1600 was quite different from the nation-state system in 1800 and enormously different from the nation-state system in 2000. In 1600, the Netherlands was one of maybe 15 pint-sized nation-states crammed into a small corner of northwestern Europe with a barely Copernican understanding of the universe. In 1800, Great Britain was one of 40 or 50 European nation-states loosely reaching across the globe with months-long voyages between continents. In 2000, the United States is one of 192 nations densely enmeshed in a net of tens of thousands of transnational corporations, nongovernmental organizations, and instantaneous global communication, and a scientific enterprise that is reading and rewriting our very genome. **Things are very different now.**

PHILLIPS ISSUES A HEARTFELT denunciation of the "political establishment" for not telling the full complex story of America's oil history and the coming global oil shortage. This, I feel, is rather unfair, because in our system, abounding with freedom of the press and energetic journalists and historians, there is no shortage of truth-tellers willing to expound on oil history at great length. It's not the political establishment's job to morph into a bunch of oil historians. You might say it's the political establishment's job to present us with "deciders" who offer comprehensible rationales for different paths.

IN THE SECTION ENTITLED *The Dead Hand of Yesterday's Success,* Phillips provides a concise history of "what made and then unmade" Dutch ascendancy in wind and winter in the 17th century and British ascendancy in coal from the Seven Years' War to the First World War.

In the Dutch story, I found particularly interesting the suggestion of a Protestant connection between the redemption of flooded land, the redemption of doomed souls, and the redemption of the Netherlands from Spanish Catholic rule. Those are interesting themes for anyone interested in religion and American history! As a matter of fact, my maternal grandfather is descended from French Huguenots, and the family name is "Lamar", or "the sea."

PHILLIPS'S EXPLANATION FOR THE DECLINE OF DUTCH ASCENDANCY is less satisfying. Essentially, he tosses up a few theories that have been offered by specialists in Dutch history and lets the reader choose for himself. He notes that in the mid-1700s many Dutch became "reoriented" towards investments rather than engineering; this certainly has a familiar ring for anyone familiar with American business history. Unfortunately, Phillips fails to offer an explanation for decline that relies on the condition of the "energy infrastructure" that is Phillips's prime concern. I do see a way to rescue his argument, though: it seems to me that one could argue that by the mid-1700s the Netherlands had exploited most of the "low-hanging fruit" from investments in wind and water technologies – that they had built all the windwills and dikes that were cost-effective.

PHILLIPS DOES A MUCH BETTER JOB of showing that Britain's early success as a coal innovator ironically created a situation in which by 1914 its "huge investment in plants, equipment and early techniques" left it with what the historian Correlli Barnett neatly described as "a working museum of industrial archaeology."

HARVARD BUSINESS SCHOOL PROFESSOR CLAYTON Christensen makes a very similar argument in his best-selling book *The Innovator's Dilemma,* the gist of which is that big successful companies that have mastered a technology have a very difficult time dealing with "disruptive technologies" that call for fundamentally different investment strategies.

It was interesting to me that Phillips does not mention here that Correlli Barnett is also well known as a historian of the Royal Navy in World War Two: a war the British Navy won through its command of next-generation oil technology. It seems to me that one could argue that Great Britain actually did a pretty good job of managing the transition from the coal era to the oil era, at least until the blunder at Suez in 1956. *Is there a Suez in America's future?* Phillips thinks so...

(Incidentally, **Iraq is not our Suez.** For those who are shaky on modern history, in the Suez crisis of 1956 Great Britain and France intervened militarily to try to prevent Egypt from nationalizing the Suez Canal. They were stunned when the U.S. failed to back their play, and had to withdraw in a humiliating manner in a matter of weeks. For Iraq to be similar to Suez, we would have had to bail out of Iraq a lot faster than we have so far. There's no "Uncle E.U." in the background for us, either.)

ARGUMENTS ABOUT NATIONAL DECLINE TEND TO FOUNDER when the question is asked, what exactly is so bad about suffering a historical decline? There are many people today who would prefer to live in the Netherlands or the United Kingdom than in the United States, including most Dutch and British people and not a few Americans.

Phillips wants us to worry about the American decline, but I'm not sure he has made that case yet.

THE FIRST MAJOR POINT that Phillips makes in his discussion of *The Aging American Energy Infrastructure* is that the U.S. oil industry is **old as dirt**. This is plausible to anyone who remembers "Giant" and "The Beverly Hillbillies," to say nothing of Spindletop (1901).

NEXT, PHILLIPS ROLLS OUT THE HUBBERT PEAK, the argument by American geologist M. King Hubbert that American and World Oil Reserves would reach an inevitable peak in a predictable, finite amount of time. Although there is no question that U.S. oil production peaked some years ago, there is some debate as to exactly how soon global oil production will peak.

For those who want to know more about the Hubbert peak here are a couple of useful images gathered from Wikipedia.

Figure 2. Hubbert peaks for the nations of the world

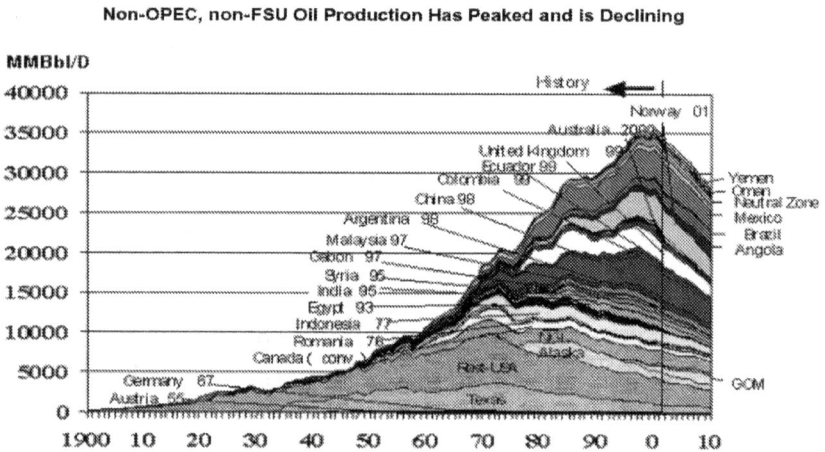

Non-OPEC, non-FSU Oil Production Has Peaked and is Declining

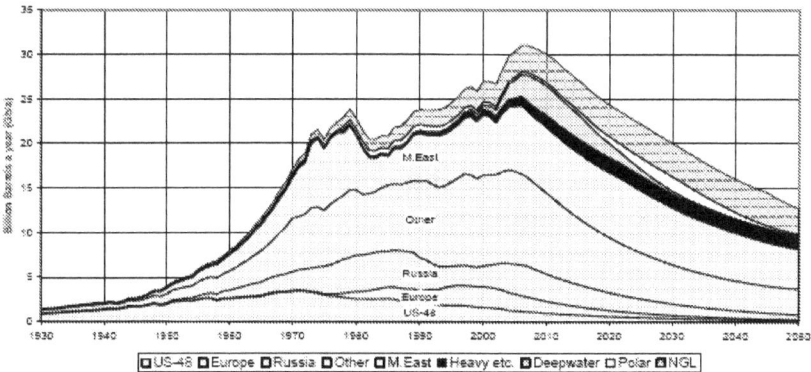

Figure 3. Hubbert peaks by continent[5]

Although Phillips nods to the possibility of improved extraction techniques and larger-than-expected reserves, the fundamental theme of his assessment is that eventually, at a time within living memory, global oil production will peak, and then run out.

SO WHAT? One thing that is missing from Phillips's discussion is the fundamental economic concept of **substitution.** As oil prices rise, buyers will tend to substitute other sources of energy, won't they? To fully justify the most frightening scenarios, Phillips must make the case that somehow the process of substitution will not work in the case of energy. **There are things in this world that are much less fungible than energy.** For example, as Peter H. Lindert pointed out in an article by Daniel Altman in *The New York Times* called "What to Do When the Oil (Or the Innovation is Gone", **"the long-run scarcities are for human labor and land."**

ANOTHER THING THAT IS MISSING from Phillips's discussion is the concept of **technological surprise.** After living through a century of enormous scientific and technological surprises, it should be

---

[5] http://en.wikipedia.org/wiki/Image:ASPO_2004.png

obvious to everyone that there may be more in store. It's certainly possible (although by no means certain!) that there may be a technological surprise in store that completely rewrites the energy equation.

I WAS ALSO DISAPPOINTED that Phillips did not mention or acknowledge the minority view that oil is **abiotically generated** by geologic processes within the Earth's crust (as opposed to biological decay of fossils, thus "fossil fuels").

From what I've read, the abiotic theory is **probably wrong**, but it is not complete quackery; there was a major article by Thomas Gold in *Scientific American* a few years back and a casual Internet search turns up an ample bibliography of peer-reviewed articles.[6]

NO CROCODILE TEARS WILL BE SHED HERE FOR EXXONMOBIL AND CHEVRON, which Phillips describes as "embattled oil giants" fighting valiantly against differently advantaged national oil companies like Petroleos de Venezeula Pemex, and Saudi Aramco who enjoy the benefits of owning their own oil reserves. On the one hand, Phillips describes the four corporate "supermajors" (adding BP and Royal Dutch/Shell) as oil-impoverished outsiders scrabbling desperately to replace their dwindling oil reserves, each barrel coming harder than the last. On the other hand, he portrays them as the lucky beneficiaries of the ultimate government boondoggle, an Iraq war that gives them control over four hundred billion barrels of crude (28 trillion dollars worth at today's prices). Phillips isn't exactly saying that ExxonMobil and Chevron are loser companies, but he's distinctly giving the impression that they have

---

6

http://en.wikipedia.org/wiki/Abiotic_petroleum#Peer_reviewed_journals

a lot of baggage and that they are far from the best standard-bearers for the U.S. population's energy future.

On that, I agree... but I don't see that the U.S. future would be brighter if our energy flagship was Saudi Aramco instead of ExxonMobil. Oil wealth in most of the countries with huge oil assets has bred hugely inefficient human capital. I'd rather have us be smart and resource-poor than lazy and energy-rich. And of course, we're not really resource-poor.   We are a continental power with immense reserves of coal, to say nothing of untapped offshore wealth and all the resources that we can tap through our global hegemony and through the magic of the free market.

PHILLIPS DROPS ONE FACTOID that's so staggering I simply had to investigate it further. He says that the Global Policy Forum's estimate of the "most probable annual profits" for oil companies in Iraq is **$95 billion,** or three times the $35 billion 2002 profits of the world's five largest private oil companies in 2002.

Let's look at this factoid in a couple of different ways.   First, its inherent plausibility. If, as calculated above, Iraq's oil reserves are indeed worth $28 trillion, and we draw them out at an even rate every year for a hundred years (not how it would actually happen, of course), and assume oil prices stay at a real $70/barrel, that's $280 billion dollars in revenue per year. $95 billion profit is a 25% margin, which I suppose is within the bounds of feasibility. Of course, if you make the drawdown period 50 years, then that's $560 billion in revenue/year, which makes it much easier to hit your profit target! If you assume 5% real growth/year in the value of oil, and treat revenue like an annuity, it's even easier to justify the theoretical profits.

How much money will the supermajors to spend in Iraq before they can make the Iraqi fields profitable?   Just off the top of my head, does a trillion dollars sound too high?   Maybe – that's $50 billion/year for 20 years ... how about five billion a year for 10 years, or $50 billion? No one knows the details, **but it's going to cost a**

whole lot of money. And of course, there's absolutely no guarantee that the investments will pay off, since there's always a chance that a hostile government will take over.

How much risk are the supermajors taking in Iraq? **How high is up?**

When you start factoring in the huge risk and investment factors, $95 billion still sounds like a lot of profit per year, but **maybe not quite so heinous.**

Now let's look at the actual plausibility of the factoid. How much money are the supermajors making in Iraq right now? **Not a whole lot,** I would say. How much money is anyone going to make in Iraq until there is a stable, efficient government? **Not a whole lot.** Are they anywhere close to realizing $95 billion/year in oil profits from Iraq? Nowhere near. So what we have in this $95 billion factoid is **a prediction that is, so far, completely incorrect.**

And let's play a quick game of "consider the source." As soon as I read the words "Global Policy Forum," I had a pretty good idea what I was going to find when I looked into the organization, and I was not disappointed when I surfed my way to their website.

> Global Policy Forum's mission is to monitor policy making at the United Nations, promote accountability of global decisions, educate and mobilize for global citizen participation, and advocate on vital issues of international peace and justice.
>
> Staff
>
> Executive Director James Paul heads the GPF staff. Céline Nahory serves as Security Council Program Coordinator and Katarina Wahlberg works as Coordinator of Social & Economic Policy programs.

James Wong acts as computer systems administrator.
Interns and volunteers from many countries give
vital support to the regular GPF staff. Jens
Martens is Director of the European Office.

Board

Joel Krieger, Professor of Political Science,
Wellesley College, serves as chair of GPF's
eleven-member Board of Directors. Other members
are: real estate executive Karen Backus,
professors Margaret Burnham and Paul Chevigny,
lawyer Devaleena Das Ullah, NGO leaders Peter
Davies and Catherine Dumait-Harper, professor
Diana Gordon, GPF director James Paul, policy
analyst Michael Renner and lawyer Aruna Chandra
Spencer.

In other words, the Global Policy Forum is exactly what it sounds like: a small, left-leaning, academically oriented think-tank with no particular expertise in oil.

OLD AS DIRT, THAT'S WHAT AMERICA'S ENERGY COMPANIES ARE, according to Kevin Phillips. He points out that ExxonMobil's grandparent, Standard Oil, would have been 130 years old in 2000, but he fails to mention **that Standard Oil was broken up** to prevent too great a concentration of corporate power—an inconvenient fact that doesn't wholly square with his "energy is everything" view of politics.

SO ARE THE AUTO COMPANIES: Ford and GM are 103 and 98 at this writing in 2006. I must agree, sitting here **ten miles from River Rouge and Willow Run,** that the auto companies' legacy cost structure is not helpful as we face our energy future. And Phillips is right on target when he points out that the domestic manufacturer's dependence on SUV and light truck sales makes them perhaps unusually sensitive to energy prices and disruptions.

I question, though, whether trucks and SUVs are disappearing from the American landscape any time soon. We are simply going to see a shift in the composition of the fleet as urbanites who, frankly, never should have bought SUVs or trucks return to cars. **Will there be enough of a critical mass of truck and SUV owners left in the United States to sustain two auto companies?** In the words of the state of Michigan's motto, Si quaeris peninsulam amoenam, circum spice" (if you seek a pleasant peninsula, look around you). If you are looking for truck and SUV buyers in the U.S., baby, **circum spice!**

SO, BASICALLY, EVERYTHING SUCKS: we are in a deep energy hole and Phillips believes that the only thing that will distract us from political debates about "the political dependence of the Republican national coalition on automobiles, gasoline, and drivers" is a *Wag the Dog* style foreign diversion. This is just another form of **Why Aren't They Listening To Me? Disease.**

WHY AREN'T THEY LISTENING TO ME? DISEASE (N.)

Occupational hazard for visionaries, change agents, and technical experts, characterized by deploring "their" failure to understand and elaborating ever more complex theories about what is preventing "them" from understanding.

Black-tinted glasses in a rose-colored world.

SORRY, KEVIN: AMERICANS ARE NOT ABOUT TO GET INTO A DEBATE about automobiles. We love them, and, if you have ever taken a look at the map, **we need them.** The North American continent is not Denmark. Hybrids are the only realistic option for the U.S. because car culture is in our DNA.

WHEE! MORAL EQUIVALENCE AGAIN! as Phillips closes this first chapter with a resounding reinterpretation of history: Iraq was "an attempt to turn the Persian Gulf into an American filling station..." Oh, yeah, after the Millenium Energy Crisis. Whoops—there was no energy crisis, was there? Well, what else could have prompted the invasion of Iraq? Oh, yeah: **9/11.** Not that I think Saddam had anything to do with 9/11 ... but isn't it pretty darned obvious the only reason the U.S. had the political will to invade Iraq is because **three thousand innocent American civilians were murdered on 9/11?**

It's myopic and, I think, unfair, to suggest that our motivations for invading Iraq were strictly oil related. Remember, there was a huge provocation in 2001 from the heart of the Arab world (recall that fifteen of the nineteen hijackers were Saudi citizens). There was a need to have American boots on the ground in the Middle East, to deter future adventures in providing havens for terrorists. And, most importantly, **it was essential to deny Saddam Hussein the right to strategic ambiguity** about his plans for weapons of mass destruction. U.S. strategy has been pretty consistent since the huge nuclear weapons scares of fall 2001: put full-court pressure on every potential nuclear proliferator. Tough luck for Saddam that we were in a position to effect regime change! As for the Iraqi people, we should be much more honest with them: we should tell them **we took away their sovereignty because they didn't handle it responsibly.** Memo to people of Iraq: show us you can govern yourself without selecting leaders who start wars, invade neighbors, and pursue WMDs, and we'll be glad to give you your sovereignty back!

AND THOSE FOUR HUNDRED BILLION BARRELS OF EXTRA OIL? Strictly a bonus, baby, **strictly a bonus!** Ok, so Phillips has a point ... I told you I was going to agree with him sometimes!

ADVANCING THE DEBATE:

1. No more single-factor explanations.

2. Acknowledge that the world of international politics in 2000 is vastly different than the world of international politics in 1600.

3. N must be a lot greater than 3 (where N is the number of "empires" supporting broad historical generalizations).

4. Employ the economic concept of substitution.

5. Acknowledge the possibility of technological surprise.

6. Don't whine because "they" don't see your obvious solution to the problem.

7. Don't forget that America is on the right side in the global conflict over oil and Islam. Would the world be a better place if it was run by al-Qaeda theocrats living in Saudi Arabia? That would make *American Theocracy* look like a stroll through the pleasure gardens of Kubla Khan.

8. Bear with me when I vent. ☺

The Politics of American Oil Dependence

SMART-ALEC SUMMARY: oil guys are "the deciders."

EPIGRAPHS FROM JOURNALISTS are like fleas from dogs: the suckers are an endless source of opinions utterly lacking in substantive authority. David Ignatius of the Washington Post and the BBC think oil is important in American politics: woo! Feels like I'm **inside the Beltway.**

PETROLEUM HAS BEEN A POWERFUL ENGINE OF WEALTH CREATION for both the super rich and the middle class, but Phillips takes a rather patronizing attitude towards everyone except the super-rich. "As for the millions of small stakeholders--the oil-stained yeomanry ... their contribution was to lobby hard in Cheyenne and pose for group photographs published ... as evidence of grassroots commitment."

The wealth creation that these small stakeholders accrued may not have been significant to Phillips, but it was undoubtedly significant to *them.* Remember Warren Beatty's wildcatter father in *Splendor in the Grass?* Wealth creation was also profoundly important to workers as a source of high-paying employment. Remember John Travolta's oil field jobs in *Urban Cowboy?* When I was growing up in Michigan in the 70s and 80s, the Texas oil industry was the destination for many of the "black tag people" fleeing Michigan for employment opportunities.

As Phillips correctly notes, it turns out to be profoundly important in the U.S. federal system of government that oil and gas is found in significant quantities in twenty to thirty states, because that has ensured a steady base of political support for the industry.

PHILLIPS DOESN'T LIKE DRIVERS: "Americans constitute the world's most intensive motoring culture. For reasons of history and past abundance, no other national population has clumped so complacently around so fuelish a lifestyle." Later in the chapter, Phillips mentions rather off-handedly that drivers favored George W. Bush by a 7% margin in 2004, but he doesn't explore the full ramifications of this finding: **functional people favor Bush.** I say this with full awareness of and sympathy for the many non-drivers among us. I myself did not learn to drive until I was 25 and I have known many fine non-drivers, including those who cannot drive for physical reasons. But the fact is that driving is really an essential attribute of adulthood in modern America, and the geography of the nation (as opposed to the geography of the East Coast) means that it will always be so.

TEXAS. TEXAS. TEXAS: throughout this chapter, Phillips leans heavily on the seemingly disproportionate role of Texas in modern American politics. He rolls out an impressive array of Texan dignitaries, from Roosevelt's Vice President John Nance Garner to Lyndon Baines Johnson to John Connally to the Bush "dynasty." (In sports, we don't start talking about dynasties until there's a "three-peat"...) There's no question that Texas has played a remarkably important and indeed disproportionate role over the last century. But there's one major missing element in the picture: **why doesn't anyone hate Texas?**

I live in Michigan, one of the states that has suffered most from Texas's efficiency at wielding national influence and corralling federal spending. Michigan historically ranks near the bottom in federal spending per capita, which is ridiculous considering that we are still a rather populous state that is the home of a critical manufacturing industry. But no one here hates Texas.

You don't hear people talking about "let's kick Texas out of the Union."People bitch a lot more about the Detroit Lion's thirty-year record of National Football League futility than about the thirty years that have elapsed since Gerry Ford was President. People think it's really unfair that the L.A. Lakers and the Miami Heat get all the National Basketball Association's TV appearances, and they complain that the NBA wants the "major market" teams to advance in the playoffs. From my perspective, people just don't seem to be all that exercised about Texas's unjust "'lock" on the national levers of power. Democrats are furious that the Republicans are in office, but they're not furious at Texas per se. Many of us have some affiliation with Texas, and we also realize that while there are a lot of Republicans in Texas, there are also a lot of Democrats. Animus directed at Texas qua Texas is simply irrational and self-defeating, and most Americans seem to have enough common sense to realize that. Is Texas's role in national politics really something to get upset about? I would say that Phillips musters sufficient facts to make his case, but somehow falls short anyway. Why this interesting paradox? It seems to me that the answer is pretty simple: **we really are one nation**.

MY OWN TEXAS AND OIL AFFILIATIONS ARE SUBSTANTIAL, and this is a good place to disclose and comment upon them. My mother's maiden name was Lamar and she was born in Texas, like her mother and father. My paternal grandfather was Lucius Mirabeau Lamar III, whose forebears included Mirabeau Buonaparte Lamar, the second President of the Republic of Texas. My grandfather Lamar spent most of his adult life working as an attorney for the California Oil Company and the oil affiliation was a source of family wealth. He owned a large three-floor house in the New Orleans Garden District, had mahogany furniture hand-crafted to fit his tastes, drove a Jaguar at one point, and was able to send his children to expensive private colleges (Tulane and Swarthmore). He is buried in the family cemetery in San Antonio, Texas.

My mother married a "blue collar scholar" (in my brother's phrase), my father, Bill Zimmerman, an ambitious young man from a professional family in Northern Virginia who became a professor at the University of Michigan in 1964 (which he remains to this day). My grandfather's oil money had some influence on my upbringing, in that some extra funds made their way into my parents' lives over the years, but they were scarcely oil millionaires, and my own class affiliation, like that of my brother and sister, was, I would venture to say, much more heavily influenced by the fact that our parents both have PhD's than by the fact that one set of grandparents had some oil money. I myself have no oil holdings except those shares held in my TIAA-CREF equity index funds as a fraction of the total stock market, and those TIAA-CREF funds are, believe me, at the low end of six digits.

THE MOST IMPORTANT CONSEQUENCE OF THE OIL HERITAGE IN MY LIFE has perhaps been a rather destructive **sense of entitlement.** Passed on from my mom to me has been a feeling that the money should be there to support an an upper middle class, or lower upper class, lifestyle; that luxuries should be affordable; and that, for want of a better phrase, respect should be given. These pernicious attitudes, which I have struggled to overcome, may, perhaps, be related to what Phillips describes as the "ingrained and possessive" nature of oil dependence politics in the United States: "a culture of red, white, and blue entitlement."

PHILLIPS REMINDS US that the U.S. lifestyle is roughly twice as energy intensive as those in Europe and Japan, but does not mention the fundamental geographic and climatic differences between the U.S. and those areas. I'd be much more impressed if the analysis took into account relative transportation costs and relative heating and air conditioning costs. It may be that **to bind together a people as a single nation across an entire continent is inherently energy-intensive**. Is that bad? I don't think so ...

PHILLIPS OFFERS MANY GOOD QUOTATIONS in this chapter, thanks to his mastery of U.S. political history. I particularly enjoyed the comment by Henry Demarest Lloyd that "**Standard [Oil] had done everything with the state legislature but refine it**" and

Oklahoma senator Robert Kerr's respect for "**the right of any American to be against any racket he isn't in on.**"

PHILLIPS CLEVERLY REINVENTS DWIGHT EISENHOWER as a Texas-born proponent of a motorized Army, which is true as far as it goes but raises again my concern that **context is important.** Eisenhower's real claim to fame was that he successfully managed the Anglo-American alliance against Hitler; in other words, that he enabled the declining and the rising Western hegemons to work together towards a common end. This cuts against Phillips's basic argument, that being a declining hegemon is bad. To be sure, England found much reason to complain about playing second fiddle in the Alliance. The reason Eisenhower remains a hero is that the alternative to his success, however alloyed from the British perspective, was Allied failure in Europe, which, in Winston Churchill's words, would have caused

```
          the whole world, including the Unites States,
     including all that we have known and cared for,
     [to] sink into the abyss of a new Dark Age, made
     more sinister, and perhaps more protracted, by the
     lights of perverted science.
```

NIXON COURTED TEXAS AND CHINA with almost equal energy, and Phillips's insightful discussion of the ambivalent relationship between the poor boy and the oil companies is well worth the price of admission. **Nixon, the poor boy from Yorba Linda,** grew up with oil wealth in his background, but enjoyed none of it himself. . Phillips points out that although Nixon courted Texas via John Connolly, but also took a variety of Draconian anti-oil measures such as the 1973 price freeze that would be unthinkable in today's Republican administrations.

PHILLIPS'S HISTORY OF THE 1970'S IS MARRED BY EXAGGERATION. He is correct in reminding us that there was an oil war fever of 1973-1975, when respected foreign policy periodicals were publishing all but explicit suggestions for invasion of Saudi Arabia and the Middle

Eastern oil fields. But he overreaches when he writes about "old hands with good memories" talking of a "Thirty Years War" over Middle Eastern oil. **I read the footnote:** he's referring to <u>an article in *Mother Jones*</u>[7], and the actual title is the "Thirty-Year **Itch**." It's not a bad article, and Dreyfuss makes a plausible case that the 1973-1975 hawk mentality has re-emerged, but look: **an itch is not a war.**

MY JAW DROPPED when I read about "**the rise of varying degrees of radical Christianity, Judaism, and Islam around the world**" as one of five converging forces that Phillips believes drove the history of the three decades from the 70s to the present day. What exactly does this mean? I'm sure I'll find out more as I read on, but for now, **it bothers me.**

Let's look at the details. To begin with, there is a sense in which **any religion worthy of the name is radical,** and a sense in which the use of radical is an epithet. What does it mean to call out a religion as radical?

Of course, to many believing Christians (and, for that matter, Jews and Muslims) it is ridiculous to conflate Christianity, Judaism, and Islam. One of them is correct and the others are wrong!

Even without making any religious decisions, it's still quite a stretch to talk about these phenomena in the same breath. Again, **context is important.** What Phillips calls radical Christianity in the United States is found in the midst of a thriving multicultural society; the same is not true of radical Islam.

It's also quite a stretch to talk about radical Judaism rising around the world. It seems to me that what Phillips is talking about as radical Judaism has been rising in maybe three places: **Crown**

---

[7] http://www.themodernreligion.com/terror/thirty-year-itch.html

Heights, **Brooklyn,** where the Hasidic Rebbe lived; Washington D.C., home of the American Israel. Public Affairs Committee (**AIPAC**); and Israel. Radical Judaism simply isn't a global phenomenon.

I was also distressed to find the Mackinder "heartland" concept used rather broadly in the same list of "convergences" to describe the **thirty**-nation borderlands of eastern Europe, the Middle East, and the Caspian Republics. Thirty is a lot of nations to include in one borderlands!

JUST BEFORE *Oil's Unique Role in U.S. Foreign Policy,* Phillips promises to explain "the emergence of oil and its extraordinary relationship with both American foreign policy and the nation's intelligence community." While he delivers on the first prong, making a persuasive case that, official Washington heeded the concerns of U.S. oil companies from the First World War on, he does not deliver on the second half of the promise, with regard to the relationship between big oil and the intelligence community. That's not to say that he's necessarily wrong, but he simply doesn't prove his case in the text of this section; in fact, it's almost fair to say that he doesn't even *state* a case for the connection between intelligence and oil companies.

PHILLIPS IS ALSO LACKADAISICAL IN RENDERING THE HISTORY OF OIL during the Cold War. "The fifties and sixties were to provide a relative lull; then the unique relationship between oil and government in the United States would once again take center stage." He might as well say "**My oil-centered theory of everything doesn't explain anything that happened** for the twenty-plus years between 1945 and 1973."

OIL MUSEUMS AND MEMORABILIA are interesting cultural phenomena, but I don't see where they are any more important in American culture than, say, **lighthouses, railroads, or Amish colonies;** and they are certainly quite a bit less ubiquitous than, say, **Civil War memorials, farmer's markets, and ornamental**

gardens. It feels like a stretch to use oil museums as indicia of imperial decline.

I investigated one of the organizations mentioned (and cited!) in Phillips's discussion of the oil history craze. W. R. Brice, editor of *Oil-Industry History,* was kind enough to send me a very thoughtful and detailed letter. I asked him how many subscribers he has. The answer: sixty (60). **Scale is important.**

JIMMY CARTER AND JERRY BROWN are the named political figures who come off best in Phillips's retelling of the energy history of the 70s and 80s. In this account, Carter "fired" the conservation weapon and Brown led California to "move away from nonrenewable fossil fuels." Wow! I didn't realize that we had Jerry Brown to thank for ending California's reliance on fossil fuels. Thank goodness all those cars there now run on alternative sources of energy.

UNNAMED REPUBLICANS apparently got it right when they took office in 1981 that increasing oil supply would be an effective way of reducing prices, but Phillips makes it sound almost accidental that "market forces rewarded" them.

AS SOON AS OIL PRICES FELL, AMERICANS WENT BACK TO THEIR WICKED WAYS, and Phillips does not hide his distress that George H.W. Bush enjoyed riding a Cigarette boat, that Bill Clinton kept an "AstroTurf cushion in the back of his bachelor pickup truck"(a completely un-footnoted and as far as I can tell completely unsubstantiated factoid), and that Americans discovered they liked light trucks and SUVs.

WHEE! MORE MORAL EQUIVALENCE! of a particularly noxious sort, as Phillips rewrites Saddam's invasion of Kuwait:

> "The war to expel Iraq from Kuwait was oil-
> related, undertaken in part to protect the

```
American lifestyle, as President George H.W. Bush
acknowledged."
```

Look: Saddam is a murdering thug with no democratic legitimacy; there's no **lifestyle fascism or imperial** overreach involved in denying Al Capone the opportunity to rob a bank.

In the next paragraph, Phillips rewrites al-Qaeda's attack on the World Trade Center on 9/11:

```
"al-Qaeda struck at a nation already concerned
about the economic implications of the 2000 stock-
market slide and the bounce-back of oil prices to
the thirty-dollar-per-barrel range..."
```

Look: bin Ladin is a murdering thug with no democratic legitimacy; it's wrong to discuss 9/11 as if it was simply **a blip in a struggle over the control for oil.** While it is perfectly true that al-Qaeda's strategic *motivation* for the 9/11 attacks was, by their own statement, economic in nature, it is misleading and immoral to fail to mention that the *effect* of al-Qaeda's attack was, first and foremost, the cold-blooded murder of nearly three thousand innocent people.

A PAUSE FOR REFLECTION ON MY PART as I realize that my tone is becoming increasingly sharp. I should emphasize again that *American Theocracy* in many ways a wonderful book. I am writing about the things that I disagree with because those are the most interesting things to write about[8]. It would be pretty dull if I just kept repeating "good paragraph on oil history! Good paragraph on oil history!" More substantively, I think a pattern is emerging. Phillips is a very smart guy, but he has a tendency to stretch his

---

[8] Obligatory and, alas, probably apocryphal reference follows. Winston Churchill on an editor's ban against prepositions: "This is the type of arrant pedantry up with which I will not put." http://en.wikiquote.org/wiki/Sir_Winston_Churchill

arguments too far. It's also completely misleading for him to describe himself as writing for and to Republicans. I'm sorry, but no one who regards a contributor to *Mother Jones* as an "old hand" is anything like a modern Republican, not even an antediluvian Rockefeller Republican. **Dude, you're a Democrat!**

NOT THAT THERE'S ANYTHING WRONG WITH THAT. Many of my best friends and most loved family members are lifelong, ardent Democrats. I myself, **cursed by a facility at understanding different perspectives**, have held political opinions at most points on the spectrum. And one goal of this book is to **advance the debate** by suggesting a less overheated view of the role of religion in American politics.

I MUST ADMIT, THOUGH, that another, **sometimes countervailing,** goal of mine is to be entertaining ...

PHILLIPS MOVES ONTO MORE SOLID GROUND in his discussion of *The Hydrocarbon Coalition and the 2004 Election*. Coalitions are something he really knows a lot about. He does a nice job dissecting election results and poll data. It's interesting that coal states and oil states strongly favored Bush, and that states without significant energy resources (aka **"loser states"**) favored Kerry. I mentioned earlier that drivers favored Bush; but it is also quite telling that **five out of six hybrid owners favored Kerry.**

THE CENSUS BUREAU calls urban "exurbs" of 50,000 population or less **"micropolitan"** areas. Twenty-seven of Ohio's twenty-nine went for Bush and ten of Florida's eleven. So far, so good: this is clearly important data. Phillips gets in trouble, though, when **he puts micropolitans on the couch.**

"FAMILY VALUES ARE CENTRAL," Phillips writes, "if by this we mean having families and accepting lengthy commutes to install them in reasonably safe and well-churched places." Well, that's what *you* mean, but is it what family values proponents *say* they mean?

From what I have observed, those locational factors are indeed important, but "family values" people *also* care, passionately, about the health and well-being of their *families as seen from inside.* It misses the point, and does an injustice, to describe family values people as if they were merely shopping for real estate. It seems to me that these "micropolitan" people are looking for places where **adequate parental attention can be provided** [usually, from a non-commuting parent] **and nefarious distractions are scarce.**

"Soccer moms" have become "security moms" in the new Republican coalition, Phillips believes, and it's fascinating that Gore's two-point lead among married women in 2000 became an eleven-point Bush margin in 2004. In essence, Phillips believes, Bush won because he was better at "tapping" fear—although another phrasing might be that Bush won because he was better at *responding* to fear.

Having dissected the Republican coalition, doctor Phillips now reveals that there's **an "Alien" inside the cadaver:** wacky theological beliefs that are affecting Republican views about energy and natural resources. Phillips begins explaining the views of today's theologically oriented Republicans with a scary reference to former Secretary of the Interior **James Watt,** a primary liberal boogey-man of the 1980's. If that's not scary enough, Phillips then describes Tom DeLay and Senator James Imhofe as EPA abolitionists who consider it a "gestapo." Now I don't doubt that DeLay and Imhofe have used heated and intemperate language about the EPA's regulatory excesses, but I'm also sure that their official position on the subject is quite a bit more nuanced than Phillips suggests here. To complete the process of scaring us to death about Republican theological views on the environment, Phillips comments that "Texan" George W. Bush

> "doubts evolution and global warming and believes in the Bible: the question is only one of degree."

NO, THE QUESTION IS NOT JUST ONE OF DEGREE. Believing in the
Bible does not mean that you think the EPA is the Gestapo.
Expressing doubts about standard scientific accounts of evolution
and global warming does not mean that you want to abolish the
EPA. Quit with the scare-mongering, **K-Phil!**

FOR JUST A MOMENT, Phillips gets inside the heads of the ostensible
subjects of his analysis, as he rightly begins to explain the
evangelical perspective on the environment with a nod to the
widely differing interpretations of Genesis 1:28:

> God blessed them and said to them, "Be fruitful
> and increase in number; fill the earth and subdue
> it. Rule over the fish of the sea and the birds of
> the air and over every living creature that moves
> on the ground." (NIV)

As Phillips points out, this passage can be interpreted as anywhere
from a call to resource exploitation to a call for the most
enlightened stewardship. Phillips doesn't seem to trust evangelicals
very much: he seems to think it suspicious that the Interfaith
Council for Evangelical Stewardship (whose memb includes liberal
nemesis Dr. James Dobson) believes that "human beings ... were
given stewardship to be fruitful, to bring forth good things from the
earth" (this is actually a far more eco-friendly translation than the
NIV!) He also seems to find it suspicious that a theological
organization believes the "sound theology" is "needed to help guide
the environmental decision-making process." I'm sorry, but if those
quotes are supposed to scare me, they don't ...

Phillips classifies "intense believers" into dispensationalists and
reconstructionists, who believe, respectively that energy policies
are irrelevant because the end times are coming, and that energy
policies are irrelevant because the world "must be made over
theocratically" before Christ will return. He shrewdly observes that
neither faction has energy policy anywhere on its agenda.

That's right: **the view from inside a believer's mind begins with the Bible.** Unfortunately, Phillips is sure that's a bad thing. "No leading world economic power has ever maintained itself on the cutting edge ... with a political coalition that panders to biblical [sic] inerrancy."

ADVANCING THE DEBATE: I see a less alarming view of the world than the one Phillips paints in this chapter. For example, while I fully agree that oil has been very important in modern international politics, I see it as just one of a number of important factors. I still believe that the Cold War was partly about clashing philosophies of government, not just about a brutish scramble for control over scarce resources. Because I see oil in context, I don't need to hand-wave away the parts of modern history that don't seem to have much to do with oil.

Single-factor explanations are alluring but in the end unsatisfactory. Off the top of my head, I can think of several other "single factors" that have been used with equal confidence to explain modern diplomatic history. To name only a few, the advent of nuclear weapons; the ideological clash between capitalism and Communism; and Thomas M. Barnett's concept of "connectivity." A truly satisfactory account of modern history would describe many complex, important phenomena occurring simultaneously and with quite a high degree of independence from each other. Oddly enough, this makes me feel safer than I would if I interpreted everything in terms of "who's got the oil?"

Similarly, I feel safer than Phillips's arguments would suggest because my view of the world allows me to believe that Saddam Hussein really is a tyrannical, dangerous thug, not a victim of oil imperialism, and that bin Ladin really is a mass murderer, not **a Robin Hood for the subsurface petroleum set.**

Although I live in Michigan, I trust my fellow Americans, including those who live in Texas. It's okay with me if Texas has had a lot of politicians in national office in the last fifty years. Would it be better if American politics had been equally dominated by Californians? Michiganders? New Englanders? I'm not at all sure that the **Jerry Brown, George Romney, or Mike Dukakis dynasties** would have been a big improvement on the Bush dynasty.

Nor do I throb with anger and fear because Republicans successfully assembled a winning Republican coalition in the last two Presidential election. I look at the data which Phillips presents, and I see a narrow (*narrow!*) majority of red-staters voting on the basis of reasonable views about the world. I feel okay with "security moms" making the difference in a narrow election, and I don't see where having the margin provided by, say, **self-assured singles** would be a big improvement.

Finally, it does not alarm me to see believers in Biblical inerrancy making up a significant portion of the Republican coalition, nor does it alarm me to see explicitly Scriptural views making their way into environmental policy. That's because I don't see a belief in Biblical inerrancy as an automatic guarantee of know-nothingism.

I believe that the Christian Bible is the divinely inspired Word of God and I believe the words of Jesus reported in John 14:6:

> I am the Way and the Truth and the Life. No one comes to the Father except through me.[9]

I also believe in the Big Bang, natural selection, evolution, and sustainable development. In Phillips's world, **I am a zebra** (to play off the ancient medical dictum that if you hear hoofbeats, think horses.) In my world, I am a member of the body of Christ.

9

http://www.biblegateway.com/passage/?search=John%2014:6&version=47;31;

As a believing Christian, I am not like one of those talking supercomputers in the original *Star Trek* who shuts down the first time the clever Captain Kirk presents me with a logical paradox. Rather, I am able to hold the Biblical framework of understanding in my mind at the same time that I hold the scientific framework of understanding. That is because I believe that science, like the Bible, is one of the choicest fruits of Divine creation.

Science, like the Bible, has its proper purpose, its proper place, and its proper nature.

The purpose of the Bible is to lead Christians to a personal relationship with Jesus Christ. The purpose of science is to understand a fraction of the majesty and complexity of the beautiful universe that God created 15.9 billion years ago in the Big Bang.

The place for the Bible is in the Holy Spirit-filled inner places of human thought and choice. Science is for those places where we need testable, reproducible explanations of how things in our universe work.

The Bible is not a biology textbook, and science is not wisdom.

I am under no illusions that all evangelicals are this open to the benefits of science, nor am I under any illusion that all Enlightenment liberals are open to Biblical wisdom. But it is views of this sort, I believe, that offer the prospect for genuine progress in the debate about *American Theocracy*.

In fairness, I must say that I suspect that these views are not so far from Phillips's own. Unfortunately, he does not express them in his book. Rather, he is intent on exposing and deploring a supposed contradiction between evangelical Christianity and sensible energy policy.

At this point, I was going to deploy Ralph Waldo Emerson's famous quip about "a foolish consistency" being the hobgoblin of little minds, but when I looked up the full quote in Bartleby's I noticed that it doesn't entirely support my point:

> A foolish consistency is the hobgoblin of
> little minds, adored by little statesmen and
> philosophers and divines.[10]

So perhaps the famous F. Scott Fitzgerald quote is more appropriate here:

> The test of a first-rate intelligence is the
> ability to hold two opposed ideas in mind at the
> same time and still retain the ability to
> function.[11]

The infuriating thing about *American Theocracy* is how utterly it fails Fitzgerald's classic test.

---

[10] http://www.bartleby.com/100/420.47.html

[11] http://www.brainyquote.com/quotes/quotes/f/fscottfit100572.html

Trumpets of Democracy, Drums of Gasoline

SMART-ALEC SUMMARY: It's all about the oil.

DUBIOUS EPIGRAPHS are a recurring theme in this book. First, Phillips quotes Bill Richardson, then U.S. Secretary of Energy, explaining in 1999 that "oil has literally made foreign and policy security policy for decades.... This is all clear." It doesn't seem to have occurred to Phillips that Richardson, a classic politico, may have had some self-interest involved in describing his area of responsibility as central to human history.

Next, Phillips quotes the *Asia Times* as saying that "It's no coincidence that the map of terror in the Middle East and Central Asia is practically interchangeable with the map of oil." Well, as a matter of fact, **a great big coincidence** is exactly what it is: Islamic terrorists in the Middle East and Central Asia are only important in today's world because of the **historical** coincidence that there are great big oil deposits underneath the Middle East Without that oil, Islamic terrorists would be no more significant in today's world than Philippine terrorists or Tamil Tigers.

SECRET AGREEMENTS are always popular in fiction, and conspiracy-minded history. Peter Dale Scott's unadorned assertion that there is a secret agreement between the U.S. and Saudi Arabia that all OPEC sales must be denominated in dollars **may well be true**, for all I know, but an epigraph saying so is far from proof.

THANK GOODNESS THAT WE HAVE BILL Moyers to explain evangelical Christianity to us. Without him, we wouldn't have the final epigraph, which neatly links together Karl Rove, the 2004 election, the invasion of Iraq, the Book of Revelation, and the prospect of a war in with Islam in the Middle East as "an essential conflagration on the road to redemption." It's no wonder that

47

liberals are scared to death, with this frightful prospect put before them.

PHILLIPS CALLS BUSH AND BLAIR LIARS for saying that the Iraq war was not about oil. I have no problem with acknowledging that oil policy and oil politics were an important element of the decision to go to war in Iraq. But it strikes me as unfair when Phillips argues that oil was the only motive, and utterly disregards the stated reasons for the war. **Unsophisticated thinkers** have jumped to the conclusion that because no weapons of mass destruction were found, control of WMD must have been a bogus rationale for war.

To my mind, the crucial issues justifying the war were 1) Saddam's defiance of U.S. (and, parenthetically, U.N) authority and 2) Saddam's deliberate pursuit of a policy of **strategic ambiguity** about the pursuit of WMD.

If we assume that after 9/11, the Middle East was properly considered a war zone, it was reasonable for the United States to declare that it simply would not tolerate the existence of a completely hostile, tyrannical government directly in the center of the decisive theatre. Throughout history, warring powers have only reluctantly tolerated neutrality from countries in such locations, much less active hostility.

Similarly, if we assume that after 9/11 the U.S. government became intensely concerned about the need to control weapons of mass destruction, and that furthermore Saddam was not willing to verifiably forswear their acquisition, it was reasonable for the U.S. to take the position that it would not tolerate ambiguity on the issue of whether Iraq might possibly develop WMD.

What I find offensive is that Phillips doesn't deal with these arguments about WMD and compliance. He simply says that Bush and Blair didn't talk about oil, so they were liars. That's disrespectful; we all deserve to have our positions considered at face value before the name-calling starts.

THE HUNDRED YEARS WAR BETWEEN ENGLAND AND FRANCE from 1337 to 1453 was an actual war . In the second section of this chapter, Phillips fails to persuade me that the oil conflicts between the West and the Middle East also deserve to be termed a "Hundred Years' War." For one thing, there's the inconvenient fact that the first time that the U.S. deployed "boots on the ground" against major powers in the Middle East (excepting the adventures in tiny Lebanon in 1958 and 1983) was in 1991: **year 75** of the so-called Hundred Years War (if you count it as beginning in 1916 with the Sykes-Picot agreement). Similarly, he fails to convince me that the German-aided Iraqi insurrection in 1941 was anything more than a footnote in the history of WW2.

THE THIRTY YEARS WAR FROM **1973 TO 2003** is a bit more plausible, especially since there's some nice reporting in this chapter. For example, I had not seen before that Henry Kissinger was the pseudonymous author ("**Miles Ignotus**") of the famous 1975 Harper's article calling for an invasion of the Saudi oil fields. I had also not seen before the allegation, reported in an article by Tanya Hsu, James Schlesinger approached British officials about joining in such an attack. **When we start talking to the Brits, you know we're serious.**

PHILLIPS PASSES NO JUDGMENT ON THE SO-CALLED KISSINGER PLAN, but reading between the lines the implication seems to be that right-thinking people would regard such a plan as **immoral adventurism.** There is a fundamental moral problem, though, with the current world energy situation: the countries that control most of the oil have done absolutely nothing to earn that bounty. That was true thirty years ago, and it's true today. To be sure, the "developed" economies of Europe and North America have been equally fortunate in their natural and even biological endowments, as Jared Diamond cleverly argued in *Guns, Germs, and Steel;* but the developed economies have contributed far more to the global commonweal than the oil-owning Arab countries. Humans are social primates that can tolerate many different means for allocating resources among groups, and we like lotteries; but it's hard for me to see a compelling reason, other than territoriality, for the oil resource to be controlled by a group that did nothing to create it, and has done little good during the time it has controlled it. The only real reason why the Arab peoples should and will continue to control the Middle East's oil resources is that it would be too difficult to fight a true Hundred Years' War to dislodge them. Territorial primates make very effective guerillas.

PHILLIPS'S VERSION OF DESERT STORM has some surprising distortions, which crop up again towards the end of this section. He writes, amazingly, that the recapture of Kuwait "was lubricated by deceits ... **regarding the Iraqi armored threat to Saudi Arabia** and the fabrication that Iraqi invaders had ripped three hundred premature Kuwaiti babies from hospital incubators." By coincidence, I just finished reading *The General's War,* the definitive journalistic account of Desert Storm written by Bernard Trainor and Michael Gordon of *The New York Times. The General's War,* which is deeply sourced on the basis of dozens of high-level interviews with military and political decision-makers, includes an extensive discussion of just how vulnerable the American military felt in the first months after the Iraqi invasion of Kuwait. In the early months of the build-up, the 82nd Airborne would have been an entirely sacrificial trip-wire if Saddam had chosen to continue into Saudi Arabia. Faced with a determined Iraqi armored assault on Saudi Arabia, the United States might very well have had to go nuclear. The threat was hardly imaginary or fabricated.

PHILLIPS MOVES ONTO SURER GROUND in the next section, "The Real Map of Iraq." It's a shame that his entertaining discussion of the historical cartography of Iraq doesn't include the actual maps that Phillips discusses, so I've included one of them here. The map on the following page was used in the deliberations of Vice President Cheney's Energy Policy Development Group and was released pursuant to a Freedom of Information Act request in 2003.[12] I infer from the fact that the shapes on the map are the same as these two CIA maps available[13] at the University of Texas Library[14] that the Cheney map was generated using a U.S. government base map of oil reserves in the region. An attachment lists oil companies from 29 nations that were seeking access to Iraqi oil reserves as of 2001.

I have to admit this is pretty striking stuff! But as usual Phillips relies more on vivid quotations than on traceable demonstration of fact. He quotes Canadian writer Linda McQuaig: "**it's like a supermarket meat chart, which identifies various parts of a slab of beef** so customers can see the most desirable cuts." This is a very nice quote, but it does nothing to demonstrate the exact nature of the deliberations by the Energy Task Force. The map is, in fact, pretty neutral on the face of it; it does not say, for example, "Oil Fields We Want to Invade," as Phillips seems to assume they were thinking. The fact that similar maps were generated for **pre-9/11 Saudi Arabia** and the United Arab Emirates[15] suggests, in fact, that the focus was more on assessing critical resources in the region and less on diabolical planning for immediate invasion.

---

[12] http://www.judicialwatch.org/iraqi-oil-maps.shtml

[13] http://www.lib.utexas.edu/maps/middle_east_and_asia/iraq_oil_2003.jpg and
http://www.lib.utexas.edu/maps/middle_east_and_asia/iraq_oilfields_1992.jpg

[14] http://www.lib.utexas.edu/maps/thematic.html#energy.htm

[15] See http://www.judicialwatch.org/iraqi-oil-maps.shtml.

Figure 4. Iraqi Oil Fields In Cheney's Sights Pre-9/11

WHILE I WAS LOOKING FOR MAPS, I found a few other interesting items. Here's a great quote from *Sketches in Crude Oil* [16]by John J. McLaurin (1898) via Google Book Search:

> American petroleum is a leading article of commerce, requiring hundreds of vessels to transport it to distant lands. Its refined product is known all over the civilized world. It has found its way to every part of Europe and the remotest portions of Asia. It shines on the western prairie, burns in the homes of New England and illumines miles of princely warehouses in the great cities of America. Everywhere is it to be met with, in the Levant and the Orient, in the hovel of the Russian peasant and the harem of the Turkish pasha. It is the one article imported from the United States and sold in the bazaars of Bagdad, the "City of the Thousand-and-One-Nights." It lights the dwellings, the temples and the mosques amid the ruins of Babylon and Nineveh. It is the light of Abraham's birthplace and of the hoary city of Damascus. It burns in the Grotto of the Nativity at Bethlehem, in the Church of the Holy Sepulchre at Jerusalem, on the Acropolis of Athens and the plains of Troy, in cottage and palace along the banks of the Bosphorus, the Euphrates, the Tigris and the Golden Horn. It has penetrated China and Japan, invaded the fastnesses of Tartary, reached the wilds of Australia and shed its radiance over African wastes. Pennsylvania petroleum is the true cosmopolite, omnipresent and omnipotent in fulfilling its mission of illuminating the universe! A product of nature that is such a controlling influence in the affairs of men may well challenge attention to its origin, its history and its economic uses.

This is a great example of Phillips's thesis about the expansive nature of America's love affair with oil. We were exporting oil not just to Iraq, but also to **the Grotto of the Nativity!**

PETRO-IMPERIALISM, the theme of Phillips's next chapter, is one of those interesting words whose very origin identifies the user's assumptions. It's a relatively recent coinage. The first reference in the LexisNexis database was this:

```
These running dogs of petro-imperialism gave us
    hand fatigue and gas-soaked hands to encourage
    some of us to opt for the more expensive full-
    service fill-up.
```

16

http://books.google.com/books?vid=OCLC05285545&id=uQX3QFH kOo4C&printsec=titlepage&vq=tigris&dq=petroleum+map+date:0-1915&num=50

--Miami New Times, Jan. 1, 1992

In other words, the term "petro-imperialism" began to crop up in periodicals and newspapers **shortly after the Iraqi invasion of Kuwait.** How much sense does that make? To be sure, the Iraqi invasion could be thought of as a form of *reverse* petro-imperialism, with noble Saddam attempting to redraw the imperialist map of the Middle East. I found a similar "reverse" usage in the *Times* of London in 2004, with former Peruvian President Alan Garcia attacking Venezuelan goon Hugo Chavez:

> Garcia has made no secret of his disdain for
> Chavez, whom he has accused of "petro-imperialism"
> – using Venezuela's oil wealth to wield undue
> influence over poorer countries.[17]

I think it's telling that the term "petro-imperialism" seems to be equally applicable when used in *reverse* of its intended meaning.

The term does not have a huge amount of traction with the Mainstream Media: only seven hits in LexisNexis in the two years 2004-2006.

---

[17] http://www.timesonline.co.uk/article/0,,2089-2200493,00.html

Documents by date

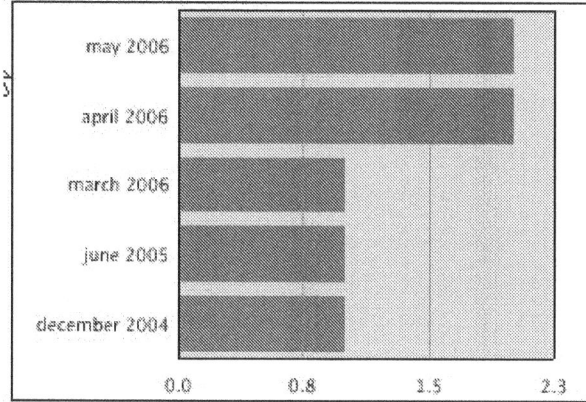

Figure 5. **Petro-imperialism in LexisNexis (courtesy Rich Miller)**

It seems to be doing a bit better in the web at large: 959 hits on Google and 22 on Google Blog Search.

PETRO-IMPERIALISM AS A CONCEPT requires equating older, explicit empires with today's modern American hegemony. In my mind, this approach is already problematic because it requires making a conscious decision to ignore obvious inconsistencies between America in the 21st century and Spain in the 16th Century or England in the 19th Century.

- In the purest sense of the word, an empire is a dominion of a king over other kings. The United States does not have kings, and (for the most part) neither does the modern world.

- The United States does not claim sovereignty over the countries that are supposed to be part of its empire.

- The United States founded the United Nations, an institution that makes today's context fundamentally different from the context in which empires flourished.

- The United States is the most important nexus of the international economics and communications systems, two more institutions that make today's context fundamentally different.

It seems to me that our hopes of advancing the debate are better if we begin by acknowledging--as we usually learn to do **in kindergarten**—that **"some of these things are not like the others."** The United States is a superpower that exerts influence over the world in a myriad of ways never imagined by empires of the past—but it is *not* an "empire."

PIPELANISTAN, the most interesting idea in Phillips's discussion of petro-imperialism, comes from a 2002 *Asia Times* article by Pepe Escobar:

> The Caspian states hold at least 200 billion barrels of oil, and Central Asia has 6.6 trillion cubic meters of natural gas just begging to be exploited. ... The only export routes, for the moment, are through Russia.
>
> So most of the game consists of building alternative pipelines to Turkey and Western Europe, and to the east toward the Asian markets. ...
>
> It's enlightening to note that all countries or regions which happen to be an impediment to Pipelineistan routes towards the West have been subjected either to a direct interference or to all-out war: Chechnya, Georgia, Kurdistan, Yugoslavia and Macedonia. To the east, the key

```
problems are the Uighurs of China's far-western
Xinjiang and, until recently, Afghanistan.¹⁸
```

Oddly, Phillips does not mention Escobar by name, although a cursory search reveals that Escobar has a remarkable record of thought-provoking essays well worth investigation by the curious reader.[19] Perhaps Escobar's online publicity photograph, which makes him look like a cross between Osama bin Ladin and Fidel Castro,[20] hints at the reason for Phillips's strategic omission.

CENTCOM, EURCOM—AND OILCOM? Phillips asks, and answers "yes": in his world view, the U.S. military is increasingly becoming nothing more or less than what Michael Klare calls "a global oil-protection service."

There are a few military angles that Phillips misses here. First, and not really trivially, force commands are geographically based, and by law the line of command runs through the theatre commands, not through any "thematic" commands. By law, theatre commanders-in-chief are responsible for all issues in their area of responsibility, so there is a balancing mechanism built in.

Second, he is ignoring the entire post-Vietnam culture of the American military. **The Powell doctrine** may have been temporarily eclipsed by the leading role of a group of highly

---

[18]

http://72.14.203.104/search?q=cache:5viFgDtgMvMJ:www.atimes.com/c-asia/DA25Ag01.html+asia+times+pipelanistan&hl=en&gl=us&ct=clnk&cd=2&lr=lang_en

[19] *The Best of Pepe Escobar,* Asia Times OnLine. http://www.atimes.com/atimes/others/Escobar.html

[20] Take a look: http://www.atimes.com/images/f_images/pepe-mug.gif .

experienced civilian right-wingers in the Bush Administration but protecting the lives of soldiers remains a top priority for America's military leadership. Tragically, this was still the case even three months after 9/11, when we had Osama bin Ladin cornered at Tora Bora but the military relied on Afghan proxies instead of risking heavy American losses attacking a fortified mountain. No matter what Kevin Phillips thinks and no matter what the civilian leadership wants there are a lot of American flag officers who are **not prepared to sacrifice American blood for oil.**

Third, Phillips is missing that there is a flip side of the oil protection racket, and, actually, this is a point that strengthens his argument. Phillips does not appear to be aware that the **U.S. Navy and Air Force would make a dynamite tool for denying oil to China** or any other hostile power. A few U.S. subs and precision guided missiles could completely interdict all oil tanker traffic to China—and that scares the Chinese a lot, because their economic and political system is if anything more dependent on easy access to oil than ours. Without economic growth, China is a chumpy Maoist state again.

WHY DOES THE WORLD NEED AN OIL PROTECTION FORCE? Phillips tap dances around this issue a bit, referring to "medieval" cultures in the Arab world and the corrosive effect of oil wealth on national elites elsewhere. Let's be clear: an oil protection force is needed because there are a lot of countries where greedy thugs trump the rule of law. **The oil protection force isn't the problem, the greedy thugs are the problem.** Not that we in the developed world don't have our full share of greedy thugs, but we have checks and balances to keep them mostly under control.

5, 4, 3, 2, 1: in the final section of this chapter, Phillips explains the decision to go to war in Iraq by identifying five more or less concurrent countdowns or "endgames" that focused pressure through the Bush administration. After eight pages of working this theme, Phillips appears to get a bit discouraged and candidly tells the reader:

> By this time, the reader may find the notion of countdowns hard to follow.[21]

This is another instance (as in the discussion of maps earlier) which I think Phillips was poorly served by an excessive editorial adherence to the standard book publishing model of **paragraphs of text in an endless flow**. Phillips's list of five countdowns would have been far easier to follow if it had been presented in table style with the countdowns numbered.

Table 1. The Countdown Crisis simplified.

Countdown.	Constituency
The peak of global oil production.	"[O]il geologists and ... some thinkers in Washington."
The end of huge profits for big oil companies.	The oil industry.
The dollar's monopoly on oil pricing.	"A handful of Americans."
Abrupt climate change in the period 2010-2020.	Climatologists and the Pentagon's Office of Net Assessment.
Armageddon.	"20 or 30 percent of Christians."

ONCE AGAIN, SOME OF THESE THINGS ARE NOT LIKE THE OTHERS. To begin with, the looming (or possible) crises run on very different timelines.

The peak of global oil production outside OPEC (important qualifier added by Phillips!) has not yet occurred, but, barring

---

[21]*American Theocracy* at 95.

technological or geological surprise, there does seem to be an expert consensus that the peak may well occur within five or ten years.

Unless you are a "rapture-ready" Christian, it is probably hard to believe that there will ever be an *end* to huge profits for oil companies, but it's certainly easy to envisage that they could abruptly fall on hard times.

The dollar's monopoly on oil pricing could end in a matter of days whenever there is a sufficiently dire economic and political crisis, such as, for example, a war with Iran.

Abrupt climate change is not at all likely to occur in the spectacular way it does in the movie *The Day After Tomorrow,* but some voices argue that we are already beginning to suffer its unhappy effects with hurricanes and even a global surge in volcanism caused by less ice weighing down the magma.

According to the Bible, Armageddon will most likely be preceded by months or years of "signals."

One of the things that is striking about these constituencies is that they are very different in size. On one end of the scale, there are "20 to 30 percent of Christians" concerned about the Biblical end times—a large number of people, surely in the tens of millions. On the other end of the scale, according to Phillips, there are "a handful" of people worried about America's debt crisis.   By Phillips's numbers, that would suggest **a ratio of 10 million to 1 of credulous Christians to prudent policy wonks.** Of course, the number of Americans who are concerned about prudent fiscal policy is very large. Phillips, as an ancient Republican, should remember that back in the day, the Republicans were the policy of fiscal prudence.

PHILLIPS REFRESHINGLY ACKNOWLEDGES that the evidence damning the oil companies as **latter-day Krupps** is not entirely definitive;

he cites "a progressive-tilting" (and thus credible?) analysis to the effect that the large U.S. firms were "torn between greed and fear" and didn't necessarily want the Bush administration to do anything risky. Now, that sounds like familiar corporate thinking ...

THE NATIONAL REPUBLICATION COALITION, Phillips says, is now composed of three major groups:

> "... energy producers and conspicuous (mostly auto-driving) energy consumers; ... wealth holders and financiers; and fundamentalist, Pentecostal, and evangelical Christians..."[22]

Apparently, only "a handful" of this subset of Republicans is worried about debt.

PHILLIPS SHREWDLY POINTS OUT that these three major groups "respon[d] ... to very different levels of candor, economic greed, and biblical preoccupation," so the five constituencies mentioned above have a tricky time tweaking their message so it is acceptable to all these groups at the same time. "Invading Iraq to ... help ExxonMobil ... would misfire in Pentecostal Assemblies of God." **Fair enough;** it probably would.

IF EVEN ONE OR TWO OF THESE COUNTDOWNS CULMINATES SOON, Phillips argues, the United States will be **in deep trouble.** He's afraid we might see all four of the "secular" countdowns culminate in the same period around 2010. The basic thrust of his argument is that the invasion of Iraq was caused by people (Republican people, that is...) panicking over the five countdowns and **pressing for action in the Middle East.**

REPUBLICAN RECEPTIVITY TO SCRIPTURE is part of the problem, Phillips believes. He cites disapprovingly Senator James Imhofe's 2002 comment that "I don't believe there is a single issue we deal

---

[22] American Theocracy at 89.

with in government that hasn't been dealt with in Scripture," as if this comment somehow proves that crazy right-wingers pushed to invade Iraq on the basis of what they read in the Bible.

Almost thirty years ago, the journalist Henry Fairlie, who was a self-described social democrat of the European variety, wrote a wonderful book called *The Seven Deadly Sins Today* (University of Notre Dame Press, 1979). In it, he explained that the ancient concept of sin provides a unifying view of human nature that can provide great insight even for nonbelievers. In this view, humans are inherently prone to sin, and it is only through God's grace that we can be redeemed. (Another way of saying the same thing is to say that we are primates whose genome predisposes us to be torn, always, between selfish and unselfish choices.) If you believe that people sin, and that government is of the people and by the people, and that the Bible has something useful to say about sin, then Imhofe's comment makes more sense. Since every issue in government involves making choices, by definition, and Scripture is all about how to make wise and God-fearing choices, in Christian ears Imhofe's comment becomes innocuous, and almost trivial.

Now, I don't rule out the possibility that Imhofe in fact meant something quite a bit more aggressive and irrational than what I imply above; but the plain words of his comment simply are not as far out as Phillips makes them out to be. Indeed, Phillips closes this third chapter with quite a few scary anti-Christian references... he invokes the dreaded *Left Behind* series, anti-Saddam videos, and a poll showing that "[n]early one-quarter of Americans polled in 2002 even believed that the Bible had predicted the events of September 11, 2001." Those must be Americans who don't know their Bible very well, because I guarantee you that the **Book of Revelations says nothing about 767s.** But Phillips is pretty darned worried about those poll respondents.

ADVANCING THE DEBATE: For those who seek to create a deeper understanding of the relationship between American democracy, foreign policy, and oil, as discussed in this chapter, I suggest the following:

1. Forget about Phillips's list of countdowns, for two simple reasons:

2. Phillips's list of favorite secular countdowns is subject to the same conceptual problem as the religious countdowns he dislikes: **if the big event doesn't happen on schedule**, that doesn't necessarily mean the issue isn't important.

3. Despite Phillips's effort to inflate the value of the countdown factors that pre-existed 9/11, it's pretty clear to me that **the war with Iraq wouldn't have happened without 9/11,** which was, therefore, the single most important driver for our Iraq policy.

4. **Don't blame the victim.** If the United States (and, by the way, the rest of the developed world) needs and benefits from an oil protection force, that's not a negative against us; that's a negative against the greedy, lawless thugs who would otherwise hold the world oil supply hostage at gunpoint (as Saddam Hussein did in his **invasion of Kuwait** in 1990).

5. **Quit calling America an empire;** reserve the term, and all flavors of the words "imperial" and "imperialism," for the hundreds if not thousands of countries in recorded human history that have actually called themselves empires and been governed by a "king of kings" whose job description reads "Emperor", not "democratically elected head of government." The word "hegemon" is colorless, but it's a lot closer to accurate; and even that is a bit of

an exaggeration. In the 21st Century, **nations aren't frogs** that jump at American bidding. We have finite resources of influence, and we have to spend something for everything we get.

6. **Don't be scared of Scripture.** This should speak for itself, and perhaps it does; more on the subject in the next chapter.

Radicalized Religion: As American As Apple Pie

SMART-ALEC SUMMARY: A lot of sects is a bad thing.

WHERE IS THE BIBLE in this chapter's three epigraphs about "radicalized religion" in America?   Instead, Phillips uses three academic works to establish his major themes for this chapter.

Roger Finke and Rodney Stark are quoted to the effect that since 1776 "upstart" sects have steadily grown as "mainline" American denominations have declined.[23]   It's interesting that Phillips gives the title of their book, *The Churching of America,* without providing the subtitle: *Winners and Losers in our Religious Economy,* which **is a giant red flag that their analysis is probably from an untheological perspective.**   It should be obvious that the mysterious workings of the Holy Spirit in the Body of Christ (as the Bible tells believers to think of the world church) are not best understood through the prism of business logic or quantitative economics.

(It should be obvious, but it is not; even many evangelicals make the mistake of talking as if the growth of Christianity is all about headcount.)

R. Laurence Moore's *Religious Outsiders and the Making of Americans* is quoted, rather redundantly, to make the same point: that small sects have always grown faster than denominations "then viewed as large and stable." Well, duh: isn't this like saying that small companies grow faster than large companies? No one can

---

[23] If you don't like the word "sects", see the discussion at the end of this chapter in the section on **ADVANCING THE DEBATE.**

grow at 20% year over year forever; **eventually the law of large numbers takes over.**

Finally, Mark A. Noll's *The Old Religion in a New World* is quoted to make the very sensible point that "the spread of American influence around the world has meant that American versions of the nature, purpose, and content of the Christian faith have also spread widely." As we will see, though, this is a bit misleading: Phillips is not concerned so much with the nature of American Christianity abroad as he is with the nature of American Christianity at home.

RELIGIOSITY IS A LIABILITY to the nation, Phillips says as he begins this chapter's narrative. It is hard to imagine a more sweeping assertion, or a more arrogant one. One must wonder: **who asked you?** And what makes you think it really makes any sense for any single individual to set himself up as the judge of whether religiosity is an "asset" or a "liability" in an abstract and arbitrary calculus of great power politics?

INTENSE RELIGIOSITY IS *BAD* in Phillips's scheme of things, as he quickly makes evident through his choice of words.

Table 2. Words and phrases used to describe American Christianity in the first three pages of chapter 4 of American *Theocracy*.

"radical" (100)
"combative" (100)
"Some message has always had to be ... punched" (100)
"emotionalism" (100)
"eccentricities of quaking, shaking, and speaking in tongues" (100)
"wild-eyed invocation of dubious prophecies ..." (100)
"religious excess" (100)

"militantly anti-modernist" (101)
"half-baked preaching about the rapture" (101)
"a toxin" (101)
"the spiritual equivalent of a shopping mall" (101)
"juggernaut status" (101)

Almost more striking are the words that Phillips strategically omits. He approvingly quotes a long passage from professor Charles Kimball, but only reveals the *title* of Kimball's book in the endnotes three hundred pages later: ***When Religion Becomes Evil.***

THE CENTERPIECE OF CHAPTER FOUR IS FIGURE 1, at page 102, which provides a variety of **impliedly alarming statistics** about what Americans believe. According to reputable national polls cited by Phillips, 83% of evangelical Protestants believe the Bible is literally accurate, 78% of all Americans personally believe in angels, 61% of all Americans believe that God created the Earth in seven days, and 71% of born-agains, fundamentalists, and evangelicals believe that the world will end in an Armageddon battle between Jesus Christ and the Antichrist.

PHILLIPS'S USE OF POLL DATA IS PROFOUNDLY DISINGENUOUS. I feel it is proper to present this harsh judgment because I believe that Phillips, as a polling expert, is certainly well aware that **there is a profound difference between what people say and what people do.** As Phillips must be well aware, the answers to surveys of this sort would change dramatically if follow-up questioning revealed unspoken mental reservations, if the questions were phrased differently, or if the questions presented (or required) real-world tradeoffs, The results would also vary dramatically if one attempted to assess beliefs on the basis of behavior: **walking the walk** as opposed to talking the talk.

> It is easier for a camel to go through the eye
> of a **needle,** than for a **rich man** to enter the
> kingdom of God. -Matthew 19:24

PHILLIPS OFF-HANDEDLY ACKNOWLEDGES that there is a large and growing secular culture in the United States, which is like acknowledging that there is a large and glowing Sun in our solar system. Has Phillips never read a daily newspaper, watched TV, seen a movie, or surfed the Internet? Has he never observed that, for better or worse, America's commercial and entertainment culture permeates not just the United States, but the rest of the world? **We're not talking about Biblical Levis here.**

PHILLIPS RUNS WITH HIS POLL RESULTS to the frightening conclusions that the United States is "the world's leading Bible-reading crusader state, immersed in an Old Testament of stern prophets and bloody Middle Eastern battlefields." ... "a biblical nation become a high-technology, gospel-spreading superpower..." "a biblically spurred great power..." He then adds the disturbing prospect that "historically, great powers have too often gone out in blazes of religious invocation," adducing the examples of fourth-century Rome, 17th-century Spain, and 20th-Century imperial Britain. As I observed in previous chapters, I am not overwhelmingly impressed by these comparisons, which rely on the morphological similarity of a great power's role in an international system whose nature and context have become exponentially more complex in the last hundred years.

PHILLIPS APPROVES OF THE MAINLINE DENOMINATIONS—Methodist, Episcopal, Presbyterians, and Church of Christ Congregational—but his own data shows that the term mainline can only be applied to them in a historical sense. In the second section of this chapter, *The Sect-Driven Dynamic of American Religion,* Phillips is intent on showing that a trend towards fragmentation is an essential characteristic of American religious history. In fact, Phillips reports that one single Baptist denomination, the Southern Baptist Convention, has 40 million adherents to the combined 15 million of Phillips's **four favorite fuddy-duddy denominations.** I apologize for the joking tone of disrespect to the "mainline" churches, but the exaggeration is necessary to make the point. There are good reasons why those historically "mainline" denominations have lost adherents steadily for decades, and **it's not just about the sects.**

PHILLIPS TAKES US ON A BRIEF TOUR OF AMERICAN DENOMINATIONAL HISTORY in the third section of this chapter, *The Ever-Expanding American Revival Tent.* As the reference to the "revival tent" might suggest, he doesn't seem to think much of the openly emotional tone of 18th-and 19th-century revival meetings involving "swaying, crying, swooning..." (108) and "falling," "dancing," and "barking" (110). Evangelicals will be offended by his inclusion of Seventh day Adventists, Mormons, and Jehovah's Witnesses under the heading of Christian sects; evangelicals normally regard those religions as non-Christian because they explicitly avow non-Biblical sources of divine revelation.

IT IS FASCINATING TO READ ABOUT THE HISTORY OF SECTS, but not, perhaps, as fascinating as it is to actually **take part in sects.** Unfortunately, Phillips's discussion of the sectual dynamic in American churches is short on empathy and insight into what sects have to offer to sincere believers. For example, I am familiar with two of the denominations Phillips discusses—the Christian and Missionary Alliance (at 112) and the Calvary Chapels (at 119).

CMA is focused on the Great Commission:

> "All authority hath been given unto me in heaven and on earth. Go ye therefore, and make disciples of all the nations, baptizing them into the name of the Father and of the Son and of the Holy Spirit: teaching them to observe all things whatsoever I commanded you: and lo, I am with you

```
always, even unto the end of the world" (Matthew
28:18-20, ASV).
```

This is not just any Bible verse, but a divine command, and these words were Jesus's last words on Earth. Is it really so radical to consider them important?

The Calvary Chapels, which Phillips describes as "California-born, charismatic, and third wave", describe *themselves* this way:

```
The most distinguishing mark of Calvary Chapel
is a servant-pastor who faithfully teaches through
the Bible verse by verse, covering the whole
council of God.
```

Again, going through the Bible verse by verse is not really so radical, is it?

If "sects" are undertaking projects that are, really, quite reasonable in theological terms, does it still make sense to think of sects as automatically "radicalizing" religious discourse in America?

PHILLIPS SAYS "YES", OF COURSE, and the way he does it is instructive. He breaks down the Christian population in America as follows:

- 25% of Americans (or 75 million of the current population of close to 300 million) are affiliated with a "network of conservative Protestant churches" that includes fundamentalist, evangelical, holiness, and Pentacostal churches.

- 15% of Americans are affiliated with the older denominations that "used to be called the Protestant mainline"

He tweaks the conservative numbers upwards by adding:

1 million Mormons

1 million Jehovah's Witnesses

An additional 10 million Pentecostals

and tweaks them downwards by subtracting the "third wave" Vineyard Churches and Calvary Chapels.

It's telling that Phillips does not carry out the computation that 1 million Mormons constitute a **less-than-terrifying 0.3%** of the nation's population. (Although Mitt Romney makes me wonder!)

As for the nation's Catholics, Phillips's basic take is that they have suffered the same **descent into irrelevance** as the fuddy-duddy denominations, and for much the same reasons. I wonder about the underlying data, though: what about migration? Surely America can expect a substantial net inflow of potentially Democratic Catholics in the 21st century.

AFTER SPENDING A FULL TEN PAGES (110-121) surveying the various American Christian denominations, Phillips characteristically reverses course and says "the point here is less to survey the various denominations ... than to sketch the revival-prone sectarian and radical side of American religion." Ironically, Phillips accomplishes his disavowed goal (surveying the denominations) but fails to accomplish his avowed goal (showing that American religion is inherently radical). scarcely radical for a Christian church to concern itself with following Jesus's commands, reading the Bible, and (like the Pentecostals) seeking to discern the Holy Spirit's promptings.

EVERYONE DRAWS THE LINE SOMEWHERE, and I would agree that adding new prophets and new books to the Bible (as the Mormons and Jehovah's Witnesses have done) is *theologically* radical. But by Phillips's own figures, those particular sects account for less than one percent of Americans.

THERE IS NO NECESSARY CONNECTION between theological radicalism and political conservatism. If, as Phillips suggests, the creation of "radical" sects is an inherent condition of American religion, there is no reason why those sects should sometimes not be Democratically oriented in political terms. Indeed, there was a great deal of such religious activity in the sixties. The fact that most liberal religious sects did not survive the 70s and 80s is simply an indictment of their underlying message, which was **weighed in the balance and found wanting** by the majority of religious Americans. (Compare Daniel 5:27).

PHILLIPS IS CONVINCING when he talks about the crucial role of religion in American elections. I have absolutely no doubt that he is correct when he writes that "ethno-religious" questions are far better predictors of voting behavior than income. (But the fact that he feels required to combine the concepts of ethnicity and religion into the **ugly portmanteau word** "ethno-religious" does tell you that he is aware that religion standing alone has some weaknesses as a predictor.)

PHILLIPS IS LESS CONVINCING when he rolls out a 1990 Oxford University Press book whose authors woke up and "discovered" that religion was important to the study of politics. Are we supposed to be impressed that social scientists were **asleep at the switch?**

I LOVED ONE INSIGHT that Phillips tosses in at the end of the section on *Religion, Politics, and War:*

> Among Anglo-American Protestants … the
> commitment to upholding liberty and freedom as …
> justification for wars … hark[s] back … from the
> English Civil War through the American Revolution
> to the American Civil War, but they always applied
> to *internal* freedoms and jeopardizes. (124)

This is a beautiful piece of historical synthesis. But I felt Phillips took the argument a bridge too far when he continued:

> That U.S. Protestant theology has now refocused
> itself on the biblical holy grounds as a
> battleground is just another of the extraordinary
> transformations taking place on account of the
> influence of religion on American politics and
> war."

It is quite a stretch to go from the unexceptionable observation that the Bible talks about the Biblical holy grounds as a battleground to the proposition that all of U.S. Protestant theology is *focused* on Armageddon.

ARE AMERICANS A CHOSEN PEOPLE? As indicated by the title of the last section in this chapter, *American Self-Perceptions of Being a chosen People and Nation,* Kevin Phillips thinks *we* think we are chosen:

> "For centuries Americans have believed
> themselves special, a people and nation chosen by
> God to play a unique and even redemptive role in
> the world." (125)

When it's stated this way, I agree with Phillips. It is certainly true that politicians, preachers, and pundits have claimed this special status for the United States on many occasions. Where I differ is that I do not agree that these words can or should be held to represent the views of American Christians in general.

The problem with Phillips's expansive thesis is that, as every Bible-reading Christian is well aware, **the word "America" does not appear anywhere in the Bible![24]** Thus, every politician, preacher,

---

[24] Not even in the **King James version!** (There is an "inside baseball" dispute about the KJV between those who still love its majesty and those who prefer modern translations based on more accurate understanding of source documents.)

or pundit who has claimed that God has given special status to the United States of America, specifically, is engaging in a degree of optimism, wishful thinking, or just plain presumptuousness, *and every literate American Christian knows it.*

Remember, the whole point of Protestantism, a nearly-six-hundred-year-old global religious movement, is that it empowers, encourages, and mandates ordinary literate individuals to engage directly with the Bible. Even the most superficial engagement with the actual words of the Bible reminds us that it is a two-thousand-year old book that does not *explicitly* discuss particular modern nations, including ours. To be sure, there are many passages of prophecy that can be read to suggest references to modern nations, but any direct linkage between the modern nation known as the United States of America and the literal words of the Bible simply *cannot* be *proven* by the text of the Word.

HOIST BY HIS OWN PETARD? Everywhere else in the book, Phillips worries about Christians taking the Bible too literally; but here he has them reading it too expansively! Which view is correct?

WHY JESUS DID NOT APPEAR, BY KEVIN PHILLIPS, hasn't appeared in book stores, either, but **maybe it should!** Phillips suggests, in jest, that someone should write such a book to detail the ... "relentless embarrassments and disappointments" of overly specific premillenial claims that have not been borne out by history. Speaking as a publisher, I agree, it's not a bad idea for a book, although the storyline suffers from having **the opposite of narrative arc:** a conflict between two tragically opposed figures rises to a crisis, then a cathartic event fails to happen, and fails to happen, and fails to happen...

PHILLIPS DOESN'T TRUST PEOPLES THAT THINK THEY HAVE A COVENANT with God. He sees them as "zealous, driven by history—risky..." (125)" The "covenanting peoples" he discusses are not likely to give modern American liberals **the warm and fuzzies:** Puritans,

Calvinists, Boer *voertrekkers,* Ulster Protestants, and Confederates. All these peoples, according to Phillips, had "supposed" covenants with God that imbued them with a self-perceived national identity as **a New Israel.** This is an intriguing theory and I gladly stipulate that, as a matter of historical fact. many Puritans, Calvinists, Boer *voertrekkers,* Ulster Protestants, Confederates, and modern Americans have believed (or at least asserted) that they were party to a special national covenant. But once, it is one thing for optimistic politicians to say that their nation is a partner in a special covenant, and another thing for Bible-reading Christians to treat such a belief as founded on Scripture.

There are many covenants in the Bible, but the one that God made with Noah after the flood is among the most important.

> Then God said to Noah and to his sons with him: [9] "I now establish my covenant with you and with your descendants after you [10] and with every living creature that was with you—the birds, the livestock and all the wild animals, all those that came out of the ark with you—every living creature on earth. [11] I establish my covenant with you: **Never again will all life be cut off by the waters of a flood; never again will there be a flood to destroy the earth."**
>
> [12] And God said, "This is the sign of the covenant I am making between me and you and every living creature with you, a covenant for all generations to come: [13] **I have set my rainbow in the clouds, and it will be the sign of the covenant between me and the earth.** [14] Whenever I bring clouds over the earth and the rainbow appears in the clouds, [15] I will remember my covenant between me and you and all living creatures of every kind. Never again will the

> waters become a flood to destroy all life. [16]
> Whenever the rainbow appears in the clouds, I will
> see it and remember the everlasting covenant
> between God and all living creatures of every kind
> on the earth."
>
> [17] So God said to Noah, "This is the sign of
> the covenant I have established between me and all
> life on the earth." (Genesis 9:8-17).

Note that this covenant was established on the broadest possible basis, not with a Jewish person, family, or nation, but with *all life on earth*. For anyone to read the Bible and think that a covenant like this applied just to their own people would be presumptuous in the extreme!

Similarly, Jesus established the New Covenant at the Last Supper:

> And he took bread, gave thanks and broke it,
> and gave it to them, saying, "This is my body
> given for you; do this in remembrance of me."
>
> [20]In the same way, after the supper he took the
> cup, saying, **"This cup is the new covenant in my
> blood,** which is poured out for you. (Luke 22:19-
> 20, NIV)

Note that this covenant again is established on a very wide basis: between Jesus and everyone who takes communion. It is implied that the New covenant applies to all sincere believers anywhere in space and time, and is not limited to a particular people or era. There is certainly no explicit scriptural reference to any other minor bilateral covenants between God and Ulster, South Africa, the Confederacy, or the United States of America.

Thus, Phillips's position, seen in the light of basic Sunday School Christianity, is that the covenanting peoples of Ulster, South Africa, the Confederacy, and the modern United States were **intensely religious, but poor students of the Bible.**

As Phillips closes this chapter, he raises the specter of the United States itself becoming **an ignorant "covenanting" pariah state like Israel, Ulster, and South Africa:**

> [t]he sense of a biblical nationhood bathed in
> blood and tribulation … now has an unprecedented
> influence in the United States as a whole. (131)

Ironically, this frightening vision of America as a self-destructive covenanting nation can only come true if a controlling majority of Americans **fail to read their Bible.**

ADVANCING THE DEBATE:

1. **Be careful in how you use the potentially pejorative term** "sect." I am not counseling that this word be eschewed altogether, because it does capture an important reality. However, it should be used with caution.

    After observing that people understandably were perturbed to have their affiliation described as a "sect" or "cult", and introducing the term "new religious movements", Jeffrey K. Haddon of the University of Virginia's *Religious Movements Page* threw up his hands as follows:

    > As an analytical tool, "new religious
    > movements" has not proven to be nearly as robust
    > as the concepts cult and sect. Putting aside for a
    > moment the question of whether the concepts "cult
    > and "sect" are critical for the advancement of
    > science, I am not convinced, that "new religious
    > movements" achieves the goals that those who
    > introduced it had in mind.

1. It doesn't communicate profoundly important information that is carried by the separate concepts.

2. Its introduction invited a proliferation of additional concepts: "new religions," "contemporary new religions," "novel religions," etc., without adding anything to the conceptual clarity. The development of science is not served when every scholar behaves as an entrepreneur with his or her own preferred terms.

3. The use of the concept "new religious movements" in public discourse is problematic for the simple reason that it has not gained currency. Speaking bluntly from personal experience, when I use the concept "new religious movements," the large majority of people I encounter don't know what I'm talking about. I am invariably queried as to what I mean. And, at some point in the course of my explanation, the inquirer unfailing responds, "oh, you mean you study cults!"

Occasionally, I feel my use of the concept NRM has provided an opportunity to make a slight dent in the shield of prejudice that blocks otherwise open and intelligent minds from understanding the fascinating phenomena of cults and sects in human societies. Most of the time, however, I feel that what I have done is substitute a word that is not known for one that is and, thus, blocked an opportunity for meaningful communication.

In my own search for a method to create meaningful communication, **I have found that telling people I study "weird" religions opens**

```
minds more readily than either the language of new
religious movements or cults and sects. When I use
the word "weird," lots of different religious
groups enter people's consciousness.
```

This perspective is not especially helpful in the context of advancing the debate about *American Theocracy!* Evangelicals will not find it attractive to describe themselves either as **weirdo Christians** or as members of "sects." Conversely, the correct theological term, **members of the body of Christ**, may not encourage constructive debate with the secular community. For these reasons, I suggest more frequent use of the umbrella term "**believers.**"

2. Don't assume that all new religious movements are radical.

3. Don't assume that it is a bad thing for a religious movement to *be* radical. The whole point of religion is that it strikes at the root of who we are.

4. Be wary of historical analogies that equate modern perspectives with those espoused by latter-day pariahs.

5. When you hear someone make a Biblically justified claim that upsets you, **open the Bible.** Don't just flip through the Bible looking for passages that support your view, or for inconsistencies that putatively invalidate the whole thing; spend some time walking in the Word a chapter at a time. The Bible is a master narrative told in sixty-six books that contain ten thousand interrelated stories. You can't hope to understand it at all unless you are at least reading some of the stories in their entirety. You need not require yourself to develop a mastery of forensic theology; it may advance the debate if you simply ask simple, open questions based on what you read.

   This approach is in line with the best principles of the Enlightenment: close reading of sources is a fundamental element of critical reasoning. It can't hurt you to read the Bible, and it should tend to increase mutual understanding and respect if you **respond to Scripture with Scripture.**

Defeat and Resurrection: The Southernization of America

SMART-ALEC SUMMARY: The South rules.

STIRRING BUT SELF-INTERESTED EPIGRAPHS are the theme for this chapter, with David Goldfield, author of *Still Fighting the Civil War: The American South and Southern History (2002)* found affirming the Civil War's continued relevance:

> "The Civil War is like a ghost that has not yet made its peace and roams the land seeking solace, retribution, or vindication."

Still Fighting the Civil War wouldn't be a very interesting book if its most quotable passage was to the effect that the American Civil War has been over for a long time!

Another "single issue voter" is Daniel Stowell, author of *Rebuilding Zion: The Religious Reconstruction of the South* (1998), who is quoted saying that, surprise, religion was an important theme of Reconstruction.

> "The primary duty of southern ministers and editors in 1865 and 1866 was to convince themselves and their congregations that God had not deserted the South...."

Don't get me wrong, this is a very interesting and indeed rather moving quote; what I find troubling is the idea of relying on a quote from an expert on religion in Reconstruction to illustrate that religion was important in Reconstruction. Experts are not always the best at providing context and balance around their work.

The third and final quote is from Paul Harvey (no, not the Paul Harvey with *The Rest of the Story)* with a classic Phillipsian exaggeration:

> In the twentieth century, with the SBC becoming
> the largest Protestatnat denomnination in the
> United States, it became increasingly apparent
> that white southerners had lost the war but won
> their peace.

Oh, really? Was slavery reintroduced and the federal government transformed into a nullity? No, of course not.

PHILLIPS TRIES TO SCARE NORTHERNERS with the vision of a Southern **"march"** (133) north to carry **"the insignia of national command"** (133). Say what? "The insignia of national command" is a beautiful phrase, but a meaningless one.

EVEN LESS FRIGHTENING is Phillips's proof point that "... Gettysburg has been rewritten as a Confederate victory by the pen of a former Republican Speaker of the House from Georgia turned historical novelist." Newt Gingrich's career as a novelist is hardly a sign of the South's triumph.

PHILLIPS ALSO CITES THE "JESUSLAND" INTERNET MEME (shown below) as a jocular illustration of increased sectional conflict, but undercuts his own argument with the comment that

> "it was in fun, but not entirely, given the
> ratio of persons in California, in Connecticut,
> and on Cape Cod who had enlivened summer and pre-
> election parites with remarks about attractive
> real estate in Vancouver or hints of relocation to
> Nova Scotia in the event of a Bush victory."

In fact, although there was a significant percentage increase of twenty-seven percent, the absolute numbers were trivial relative to the U.S. population of almost 300 hundred million: **fewer than 10,000 people** from the United States became permanent residents of Canada in the year after the Bush election.[25] So how bad was the sectional conflict, really?

Phillips is aware of the danger of exaggeration:

> "For all that flippancy about a second civil war reeked of convenient hyperbole, the sectional tension was familiar enough."

He's absolutely correct about the tension—I loved his factoid that 2004 was the first time that all nine northeastern states had voted against the winning presidential candidate—but I wish he would listen to his own advice about the hyperbole.

Figure 6. The United States of Canada and Jesusland

---

[25] http://www.cic.gc.ca/english/monitor/issue12/02-immigrants.html

ONE FASCINATING THING ABOUT KEVIN PHILLIPS is that his writing ranges so widely in probative quality, often veering from startling historical insight to laughable exaggeration within the space of a few paragraphs. This trait is fully displayed in the next section of this chapter which is devoted to *The North-South Axis of American Cultural Conflict.* He starts out with some great stuff about the split between New England Puritans ... [who] ... supported Parliament in the English Civil War ... while the plantation colonies ... of Maryland and Virginia ... took the king's side." He makes a persuasive case that this split lasted far longer than most people think, and that it morphed into the familiar north-south split over slavery and the admission of new states to the Union. I learned some interesting things here; for example, I had forgotten, if I ever knew, that southern senators cast covetous eyes on adding new states from Cuba and northern Mexico in the 1850s. *There's* an interesting counter-factual!

I loved Phillips's masterful pull-quote tour of the role of history in the postwar South:

> "the Confederacy became immortal" - Robert Penn Warren
>
> "God's chosen people (white southerners) had been baptized in the blood of suffering" - Paul Harvey
>
> "Memory itself became a battlefield" - Phillips

Phillips begins to veer off solid ground as he quotes a variety of pundits describing sectional conflict as a "second civil war." First, he cites Novak, Buchanan and Witcover at a 1998 caffee klatsch, then he cites a variety of self-interested authors quoting from their own books with titles like *The Yankee and Cowboy War* and *The Americanization of Dixie.* Sorry, but **a thousand melodramatic**

metaphors from a thousand pundits would not budge the needle of proof. We haven't had a civil war in this country since 1865, and thank God for that.

Phillips pulls out a 1986 book called *Why The South Lost* (!) and uses it to make the argument that by the mid-80s the South had achieved most of its war aims: "state rights, white supremacy, and honor" and that "the subsequent decades have been even more encouraging for southerners." Let's unpack that for a moment:

- Sure, the Supreme Court is more receptive to state's rights arguments than it used to be, but so what? **State's rights** don't seem to be doing much to help Louisiana and Mississippi recover from Katrina. The action, and the power, is still at the Federal level.

- Southerners have no formal white supremacy in law, and nothing like the informal supremacy they had before the Civil War.

- As for "honor"—that has been in scarce supply on both sides of the Mason-Dixon line for a long time.

- And, by, the way, **the South lost**.

Finally, Phillips holds up a few **wackos** like the League of the South and the Sons of Confederate Veterans, then, a paragraph later, characteristically acknowledges that the emergence of these fringe groups has no probative value whatsoever:

> Peripheral as these events may seem…

Stop right there, K-Phil! They **are** peripheral.

PHILLIPS DISCUSSES THE THEOLOGICAL HISTORY OF SLAVERY without actually printing a word from the Bible, which is a nifty trick. He does provide a few chapter and verse citations to passages in the Bible that were used by Southern ministers to support slaveholding, but it struck me as rather unfair that Phillips doesn't provide the corresponding passages used by Abolitionist ministers.

Intrigued, I spent some time researching the issue, and found that the answers were rather humbling. The Old Testament, of course, is full of references implicitly or explicitly approving the then-common practice of slavery, and there are only a few short, and arguably misinterpreted passages, in the New Testament that denounce slavery. If you're looking to the Bible as an Ordinance to mankind whose literal words outlaw slavery, you are going to be disappointed. It seems to me that the theological argument for abolitionism from the Christian Bible must be based on what the 21st century calls "a master narrative": the progress of God's relationship with man from a limited covenant with a singular chosen people, the Jews, themselves oppressed and enslaved, to a renewed and redeeming New Covenant with all of humanity, itself formerly oppressed and enslaved by sin.

The Wikipedia essay on abolition and Christianity highlights just two "anti-slavery" phrases from the Bible, but they do a nice job of summing up one version of the master narrative:

> Afterward Moses and Aaron went to Pharaoh and said, "This is what the LORD, the God of Israel, says: 'Let my people go.' (Exodus 5:1).

> There is neither Jew nor Greek, slave nor free, male nor female, for you are all one in Christ Jesus. (Galatians 3:28)

The essay about slavery and the Bible that I that I found the most insightful was by Michael Marlowe at http://www.bible-researcher.com, who declares his faith as follows:

> Theologically I am conservative and Reformed. I consider the Westminster Confession of Faith to be an accurate summary of Biblical theology.

He does a nice job of synthesizing research into the New Testament's views on slavery:

John H. Elliott has reviewed these unconvincing efforts to find an egalitarian 'historical Jesus,' and in conclusion he finds it necessary to restate the obvious:

> This concept that all persons are equal in respect to economic, social, legal, and political domains is of modern, Enlightenment origin and has been shaped by momentous economic, social, and political changes dramatically distancing our modern world from that of the biblical writers. The equality celebrated in the American and French revolutions, has little, if anything, in common with the comparatively rarely discussed concept of equality (more frequently "equity" or proportional equality) in the ancient world. Accordingly, searching for instances of egalitarianism in the New Testament communities, indeed in the ancient world on the whole, is as pointless as hunting for modern needles in ancient haystacks. [4]

As hard as this may be, it is only by prescinding from such modern cultural presuppositions and by adopting instead the presuppositions of the Bible's authors, that one can even begin to understand and respect its teachings as the word of God. As D.E. Nineham puts it:

> If God has condescended to address men in the full particularity of their peculiar

87

> historical and cultured environments, then
> we have got to immerse ourselves fully and
> sympathetically in those environments, with
> their customs and values, ways of thinking
> and patterns of imagery, before we can
> understand either his demand or their
> response. [5]
>
> Unfortunately, it is not only liberal scholars
> who refuse to immerse themselves sypathetically in
> the Bible, but also many 'evangelical' scholars.
> We are not always well served by our own
> conservative commentators and translators in this
> matter. There seems to be an apologetic motive at
> work here -- the Bible is *domesticated* in order to
> avoid scandalizing those who would be shocked to
> discover how utterly foreign it is to modern
> values.[26]

The reason these passages struck such a chord with me is that the authors' treatment of the slavery issue mirrors the larger issue posed by the book that is before you. In today's polarized "red v. blue" environment, "full and sympathetic" immersion in the minds of others is increasingly uncommon, and true dialogue seems rare indeed.

To digress for a moment along this line of thought, I found the fascinating graphic on the next page from a company called orgnet.com. Orgnet used its proprietary network analysis software, InFlow, to analyze the "bought x also bought y" relationships among the top 100 political bestsellers from Amazon.com in August 2006. As the figure illustrates, there is a lot of distance between the

---

[26] http://www.bible-researcher.com/slavery.html

red and blue readers. Most of the purple books, which are bought by both red and blue readers, are not strictly political.

From Beirut to Jerusalem
The Clash of Civilizations
The Lexus and The Olive Tree
Blink   Collapse
The Tipping Point
The World Is Flat
Freakonomics
White Guilt
America
1776   On Bullshit
Enough
Team of Rivals
Godless
Myths, Lies, and Downright Stupidity
An Inconvenient Truth
The Professors
America at the Crossroads
Unhinged
Top 10
Armed Madhouse
The Shia Revival
How Would a Patriot Act?   Cobra II
Do As I Say (Not As I Do)
State of War
The Politically Incorrect Guide to Islam
The Assassins' Gate
Hostile Takeover   The One Percent Doctrine
100 People Who Are Screwing Up America
F.U.B.A.R.   Fiasco
Why I Left Jihad
Conservatives Without Conscience
The End of Iraq   The Foreigner's Gift
The Looming Tower
American Theocracy

Copyright © 2008, Valdis Krebs

Figure 7. Blue books on left, red books on right.

In a perfect world, I'd like this book to be in that middle group, bought by both blue-staters and red-staters. But it's going to be hard to hit that target. Argumentation has a logic all its own that incents me to making points and highlighting omissions rather than nodding along. I can't spend all my time writing "yes, yes, Phillips is masterfully insightful throughout this chapter."

YES, YES, PHILLIPS IS MASTERFULLY INSIGHTFUL in his discussion of how Southerners saw themselves as a New Israel, a covenanted people redeemed by suffering, with a unique, unreconstructed regional identity. But there is **a counter-narrative of national reconciliation.** My great-great-great-great grandfather, **Lucius Quintus Cincinatus Lama**r, is featured in John F. Kennedy's *Profiles in Courage* because of the following speech, which he gave on the occasion of the death of fiery abolitionist Senator Charles Sumner in 1874.

It was certainly a gracious act on the part of Charles Sumner toward the South, tho unhappily it jarred on the sensibilities of the people at the other extreme of the Union, to propose to erase from the banners of the national army the mementoes of the bloody internal struggle which might be regarded as assailing the pride or wounding the sensibilities of the Southern people. The proposal will never be forgotten by that people so long as the name of Charles Sumner lives in the memory of man.

But while it touched the heart and elicited her profound gratitude, her people would not have asked of the North such an act of self-renunciation. Conscious that they themselves were animated by devotion to constitutional liberty, and that the brightest pages of history are replete with evidences of the depth and sincerity of that devotion, they can but cherish the recollection of the battles fought and the victories won in defense of their hopeless cause; and respecting, as all true and brave men must respect, the martial spirit with which the men of the North vindicated the integrity of the Union, and their devotion to the principles of human freedom, they do not ask, they do not wish the North to strike the mementoes of heroism and victory from either records or monuments or battle-flags. They would rather that both sections should gather up the glories won by each section, not envious, but proud of each other, and regard them as a common heritage of American valor. Let us hope that future generations, when they remember the deeds of heroism and devotion done on both sides, will speak, not of Northern prowess or Southern courage, but of the heroism, courage and fortitude of the Americans in a war of ideas—a war in which each section signalized its consecration to the principles, as each understood them, of American liberty and of the Constitution received from their fathers.

Charles Sumner in life believed that all occasion for strife and distrust between the North and South had passed away, and there no longer remained any cause for continued estrangement between those two sections of our common country. Are there not many of us who believe the same thing? Is not that the common sentiment, or if not, ought it not to be, of the great mass of our people, North and South? Bound to each other by a common constitution, destined to live together under a common government, forming unitedly but a single member of the great family of nations, shall we not now at last endeavor to grow toward each other once more in heart, as we are indissolubly linked to each other in fortunes? Shall we not, while honoring the memory of this great champion of liberty, this feeling sympathizer with human sorrow, this earnest pleader for the exercise of human tenderness and heavenly charity, lay aside the concealments which serve only to perpetuate misunderstandings and distrust, and frankly confess that on both sides we most earnestly desire to be one—one not merely in political organization; one not merely in community of language, and literature, and traditions, and country; but more and better than all that, one also in feeling and in heart?

Am I mistaken in this? Do the concealments of which I speak still cover animosities, which neither time nor reflection nor the march of events have yet sufficed to subdue? I can not believe it. Since I have been here I have scrutinized your sentiments, as expressed not merely in public debate, but in the abandon of personal confidence. I know well the sentiments of these my Southern friends, whose hearts are so infolded that the feeling of each is the feeling of all; and I see on both sides only the seeming of a constraint which each apparently hesitates to dismiss.

The South—prostrate, exhausted, drained of her life-blood as well as her material resources, yet still honorable and true—accepts the bitter award of the bloody arbitrament without reservation, resolutely determined to abide the result with chivalrous fidelity. Yet, as if struck dumb by the magnitude of her reverses, she suffers on in silence. The North, exultant in her triumph and elevated by success, still cherishes, as we are assured, a heart full of magnanimous emotions toward her disarmed and discomfited antagonist; and yet, as if under some mysterious spell, her words and acts are words and acts of suspicion and distrust. Would that the spirit of the illustrious dead, whom we lament to-day, could speak from the grave to both parties to this deplorable discord, in tones which would reach each and every heart

> throughout this broad territory: **My countrymen!
> know one another and you will love one another.**[27]

Well said.

Lest you think that I am blinded by family allegiance, it's interesting to note that a few years later, in 1877, Democrat Lamar helped Republican Rutherford Hayes secure the office of President in the most tightly contested Presidential election before 2000:

> To resolve the dispute, Congressman Lamar, who
> would soon be Senator Lamar, helped set up a
> nonpartisan Election Commission, which chose Hayes
> as president.
>
> Behind the scenes, Lamar was very involved in
> the bargaining and won many concessions for the
> South in exchange for supporting the Commission's
> conclusions. Many Southerners were outraged that
> the election had in their eyes been stolen from
> the Democrat Tilden. They were more outraged that
> Lamar was involved in the deal.[28]

Almost as if **Katherine Harris** had been a Democrat and helped Bush win the 2001 election!

The moral of this story is that it has never been easy or popular to occupy the middle ground between blue and red staters. John Kennedy liked to tell a story to illustrate the point that Senators (and by extension, other national leaders) sometimes need to go where their polarized followers will not:

> If we are to exercise fully [our] judgment,
> sometimes we may be required to lead, inform,

---

[27] http://www.bartleby.com/268/10/6.html

[28] http://mshistory.k12.ms.us/features/feature69/Roger2.htm

correct and on occasion even ignore public opinion
in our States.

I think that a rather simple, a rather "corny"
but a rather thought-provoking story once told by
a Mississippi Senator who had opposed his state
best illustrates this point. The Senator involved
bore the fascinating name of Lucius Quintus
Cincinnatus Lamar; and he had gotten himself into
the predicament of which I spoke by three
different actions: first, he had delivered a
moving eulogy in the Congress upon the death of
the South's most implacable enemy, Senator Charles
Sumner of Massachusetts; secondly, he had abided
by the decision of the special electoral
commission to award the Presidency to the
Republican Rutherford B. Hayes in 1876; and
finally and most terrible of all, he had violated
the instructions of his State Legislature and
ignored the wishes of his constituents by opposing
the free silver movement which sought to promote
easy, inflationary money for the relief of
Mississippi and other debtor and depression-ridden
states.

When Lucius Lamar returned to Mississippi he
was met with bitter hostility. But in a series of
powerful speeches which he delivered throughout
the State, senator Lamar, a former officer of the
Confederacy, told the story which I would like to
repeat to you. In the company of other prominent
military leaders of the Confederacy, he said, he
had been on board a blockade runner making for
Savannah harbor; and the Captain had sent sailor
Billy Summers to the top mast to look for Yankee

gun boats in the harbor. Billy said he had seen
ten. But that distinguished array of officers knew
where the Yankee fleet was, Lamar related, and
they told the Captain that Billy was wrong and
that he should proceed ahead. **The Captain refused,
insisting that while the officers knew a great
deal more about military affairs, Billy Summers on
the top mast with a powerful glass knew a great
deal more about what boats were in the harbor.** It
later developed, according to Lamar, that Billy
was right, and that if they had gone ahead they
would all have been captured.

And so Lamar insisted to his constituents that
he did not claim to be wiser than they; but that
he was in a better position as a member of the
Senate to judge what was in their best interests.
And he concluded the story with these words:

"Thus it is, my countrymen, you have sent me to
the topmost mast, and I tell you what I see. If
you say I must come down, I will obey without a
murmur, for you cannot make me lie to you; but if
you return me to my post, I can only say that I
will be true to love of country, truth, and God."[29]

Take *that,* **netroots!**

**THE SOUTHERN BAPTIST CONVENTION IS AN EIGHT-HUNDRED-TON
DINOSAUR,** Phillips tells us as he begins his next section. I'm not
especially familiar with the history of the SBC, so I can only

---

29

http://www.jfklibrary.org/Historical+Resources/Archives/Reference
+Desk/Speeches/JFK/JFK+Pre-
Pres/002PREPRES12SPEECHES_55OCT27.htm

counter-punch here as I observe Phillips's by-now familiar rhetorical mannerisms ("tricks" may be too harsh a word). To begin with, I observe that Phillips's dinosaur is **two thousand times bigger and 65 million years older than an eight-hundred-pound gorilla.** That's some dinosaur!

The most interesting observation I can offer on this section is that **Phillips doesn't seem to listen to his own sources!** *The Churching of America* by Finke and Stout, which is one of Phillips's prime sources for his chapter four, includes a long discussion of the Southern Baptist Convention through 1990. Finke and Stout emphasize that the self-governing congregational constitutions common in the SBC give the lay congregations a great degree of power relative to the denomination and its pastors. They also emphasize that the SBC, like every religious organization, is subject to the same waxing and waning of tension with the surrounding society that (in the United States, at least) they believe causes established churches to wane and new sects to emerge. These two points go directly contrary to two of Phillips's major points about the SBC:

> "[C]an the SBC … be fairly described as fundamentalist?"

> "[C]an the [SBC] be considered the de facto Church of the South—the closest thing to an official church in the United Sttes since the establishment of Congregationalism in New England almost two centuries ago?" (156)

If Finke and Stout are correct in their model of church and sect change, the moment that the SBC becomes dominated by fundamentalists, their new-found power will cause them to lose creative tension with "the culture", and will cause religious enthusiasm to switch to newer sects.

If Finke and Stout are correct in describing SBC as locally governed, does it make much sense to talk about SBC as being an "official church"? Especially since there is still a first Amendment that makes it clear that **there will be no official churches in the United States, ever?**

THE LAST SECTION of this chapter, *The Greater South and the Future of the Republic,* is nine pages long, but it can be summarized concisely.

- The Civil War involved more than just the southern states of the Confederacy; there was a pivotal struggle for control over the Greater South including the borderlands and the West.

- The South could have won the struggle for the Greater South and if it had it would have won the Civil War.

- After the Civil War, many people from the South and North moved to new places, and brought their values with them.

- The SBC and other southern denominations followed, and were effective at gaining adherents.

- "Two southern sociologists" think evangelical theology is "structurally racist"; nevertheless **two thousand, seven hundred (2,700)** black congregations are members of the Southern Baptist Convention (Emerson and Smith, 170).

ADVANCING THE DEBATE:

1. **Self-interested experts** shouldn't be quoted to prove the thesis of their own books. It is much more credible when someone who is a global expert on a wide domain (e.g. American history) offers a judgment on the importance of a particular issue in the context of the entire domain.

2. **We must make the effort to meet Others on their own ground.** For secular **disestablishmentarians**, this means opening the Bible from time to time. Take a page from Barack Obama's playbook! For Christians, this means acknowledging that the United States Constitution **wisely prohibits the establishment of a state religion.**

3. I appreciate Phillips's openness (mentioned immediately above) to the idea that history might have come out differently; so often historians and social scientists write as if everything that occurred in the past was **overdetermined,** rather than the emergent result of dynamic choices; I would use the phrase "game play" if it did not seem to trivialize the importance of the results. Despite what the "reality-based community" may think, **we create our own future,** one day at a time.

4. There is a lot of good history in this chapter. I remembered quite a few things and learned a lot more. **Keeping the facts front and center is a good thing.**

The United States in a Dixie Cup: The New Religious and Political Battlefields

SMART-ALEC SUMMARY: Christians have been voting Republican. **Waaah!**

PLEASE REREAD THE FOUR EPIGRAPHS ABOVE, Kevin Phillips writes, little knowing that I have been subjecting *all* of his epigraphs to intense scrutiny! This chapter's epigraphs are a good set.

The first epigraph is from Richard Land, whom Phillips describes as "chief Washington representative of the Southern Baptist Convention." (It's a bit surprising that Phillips just doesn't come out and call him a "lobbyist," but I must applaud Phillips for playing fair.) Land is quoted saying:

> "George Bush is an evangelical Christian,
> there's no doubt about that."

Land goes on to provide four "proof points" in terms of Bush's specific beliefs that are consistent with evangelical theology.

To borrow the old phrase, "if it looks like a duck, walks like a duck, and quacks like a duck, it's a duck." **43 does a lot of quacking.** I do add a caveat, though. It is impossible to truly know from the outside is what Bush's faith means to him on a day-to-day, hour-to-hour, or minute-to-minute basis. There are committed evangelical Christians who are breathed with the Holy Spirit and doing God's work in every moment, and there are committed evangelical Christians who are tragically unaware that they are being deceived by the Great Tempter. It can be difficult for even the most faithful to know which category they fall into at any given moment; let alone if you lead your life in a whirlwind of public activity and conflict.

The second epigraph, from a USA Today article, highlights the "religion gap":

> Voters who say they go to church every week usually vote for Republicans. Those who go to church less often or not at all tend to vote Democratic.

This one is easy to dispense with: **Democrats need to go to church.**

The third epigraph, from Dana Milbank at the *Washington Post,* is a classic **Phillipsian exaggeration:**

> "The President of the United States has become the … de facto leader … of [the religious conservative political movement."

You know there's trouble when you see those weasel words "**de facto.**" Have you seen the *size* of the egos on some of the less attractive right-wingers: the Jerry Falwells, Pat Robertsons, and Ralph Reeds? All those guys think they have a direct pipeline to God; do you really think they believe *any* President is **the boss of them?**

Finally, Phillips quotes David Domke, author of God *Willing,* to the effect that

> … the Bush Administration's worldview … is one grounded in religious fundamentalism. Such a worldview is disastrous for a democratic system.

This sounded like a pretty authoritative assessment until I Googled *God Willing.* It's distributed in the U.S. by my neighbor the University of Michigan Press – Go Blue! – on behalf of Pluto Press. Here's what Pluto Press has to say about itself:

> Pluto Press has a proud history of publishing the very best in progressive, critical thinking

across politics and the social sciences. We are an
independent company based in London, with a sales
and marketing office in the United States and
distribution rights throughout the world.

Pluto Press has always had a radical political
agenda. Founded in 1969 as a publishing arm of
International Socialism, the forerunner of the
Socialist Workers Party in the UK, in 1979 we
broke with this political affiliation and became
truly independent. Today, we represent authors
from a wide range of progressive political
viewpoints. With over 550 titles in print, Pluto
Press is one of the world's leading radical book
publishers…. We publish political classics by
writers including Karl Marx, Frederick Engels,
Leon Trotsky, Frantz Fanon, Andre Gorz, Manning
Marable, Jack London and Antonio Gramsci.
Contemporary political writers and voices of
conscience include Noam Chomsky, Edward Said,
Howard Zinn, bell hooks, Ariel Dorfman, Susan
George, John Pilger, Ziauddin Sardar, Israel
Shahak, Greg Palast, Milan Rai, William Rivers
Pitt, Boris Kagarlitsky, Robin Hahnel, Saul
Landau, Sheila Rowbotham, Peter Fryer, Joseph
Rotblat, Frank Füredi, Eduardo Galeano and Vandana
Shiva.

Now, the publisher's political framework does not per se discredit
God Willing. For all I know (having not yet read the book),
Domke's argument may be masterly and irrefutable. But what I *do*
know is that it bothers me that Phillips plunks the Domke quote in
there as if the source is as objective and authoritative on its subject
as the Southern Baptist Convention is on evangelical theology, or as
USA Today and the Washington Post are on American politics. The
source of this fourth epigraph is a book from publishing house

whose self-proclaimed values are so far to the left of the *American* left that they pretty much fall off the map.

Now, to be fair, it sounds like the book itself uses a reasonable and analytic methodology:

> In the aftermath of the September 11 terrorist attacks, President George W. Bush and his administration offered a 'political fundamentalism' that capitalized upon the fear felt by many Americans. Political fundamentalism is the adaptation of a conservative religious worldview, via strategic language choices and communication approaches …
>
> This book analyzes hundreds of administration communications and news stories from September 2001 to Iraq in spring 2003 to examine how this occurred and what it means for U.S. politics and the global landscape.[30]
>
> … David Domke is Associate Professor of Communication at the University of Washington. Domke is a former journalist and received his Ph.D. from the University of Minnesota in 1996.

The hidden card in this game of **three-card monte** is that the Washington representative of the SBC is probably better qualified to pronounce on "who appears to be an evangelist than an arbitrarily self-selected university professor is to pronounce on whether the Bush administration is fundamentalist and whether

---

[30] http://www.plutobooks.com/cgi-local/nplutobrows.pl?chkisbn=0745323057&main=&second=&third=&foo=../ssi/ssfooter.ssi

that's bad for democracy. Simply put, liberal university professors are **a dime a dozen.**

Now, to be fair, I've got to read Domke's book. It's not at the local library, so I just ordered a copy!

WHICH CAME FIRST: THE CHICKEN OR THE EGG? Phillips's chicken is "the southernization of U.S. politics" and the egg is the "glaring ... reorganization of the Republican party around religion." In this view:

Why did the chicken cross the road? Because it could. Ever since the Civil War the South has been on a sustained power grab.

You can't make an omelet without breaking eggs. The Republican party has reorganized itself around religion not because it wants to, but because it is cynically going where the votes are.

The remainder of the introduction to this chapter amounts basically to a recounting of history to support the proposition that the emergence of today's governing Southern Republican coalition is a rerun of the emergence of the hawkish, fundamentalist, literalist Southern coalition that started **the Civil War.** As Phillips observes rather dryly,

> "with respect to both southern belligerence and the dangers of crusading religion, this historical dimension suggests the need for great caution."
> (173)

It's fascinating that Phillips spends so much time and energy trying to scare me. I'm not worried that the Republican south is going to start a new Civil War, and **I'm not going to blame it on the South** if the Republican elected majority gets us into a disastrous war overseas. There are Republicans in all fifty states, and we are one nation.

FROM ZEROS TO HEROS: I learned in the next section, *Southerners and Republicans: The Great Reversal,* that Republicans weren't even on the ballot in any of the eleven Confederate states during the 1860 election. Now, of course, they dominate the South. What happened? Phillips traces the long arc of this change through the intervening history, but what I found most interesting is the huge spike in the curve that occurred in 1972. As Phillips's own figure shows, the Republicans did not win more than two Southern states in any of the Presidential elections from 1944 through 1968. Then, in 1972, they won all eleven. The series goes like this: 0, 0, 0, 0, 0, 2, 1, 11. The popular vote statistics were even more overwhelming: at least 79% of southern whites voted for Nixon.

Phillips discusses this watershed election without giving his full attention to one important line of explanation: the Democratic party **idiotically chose an unelectable candidate.** Does that sound at all familiar as we head into 2008?

Phillips seems to support the proposition that the Democrats brought their troubles on themselves with his observation that

> "most of the great GOP advances below the
> Mason-Dixon line came from angry white responses
> to southern and border-state Democratic
> presidencies." (181)

His argument is that national Democratic constituencies "obliged" Southern Democratic presidents to pursue agendas contrary to Southern interests. While it's hard to swallow that men as stubborn and driven as Harry S Truman and Lyndon Baines Johnson were forced to do anything, I think Phillips is right on the facts. In Phillips's reading of history, Democratic administrations consistently took positions that alienated their key constituency in the South. **Whose fault is that?**

PHILLIPS IS USUALLY RELUCTANT TO REGARD THE UNITED STATES AS SPECIAL, but he makes an exception in the next section, titled *The First American Religious Party*. *We're* special because, whereas many countries in the world have religious parties based on one particular faith, we have an "ecumenical" religious party that has "mobilized religious intensity on a multidenominational basis."

On the face of it, that doesn't sound like it's necessarily a bad thing. It's very multicultural and diverse of us, right? The problem, according to Phillips, is that over the last thirty years **a religion gap** has emerged. Phillips spends eight pages walking us through the history of the elections between 1972 and 2004. I'll just hit the high points:

- Phillips provides a great pull quote from futurist and nuclear strategist Herman Kahn *(Thinking the Unthinkable)*:

    "The biggest movement in America in the 70's is the counter-reformation … [the rise of] religions such as Baptists, Church of Christ, Pentecostals, Jehovah Witnesses and … Jesus freaks

- The irony that Jimmy Carter, a Southern Baptist and quite possibly the most sincerely devout American President *ever,* lost support from Southern Baptists.

- Phillip's shrewd point that 1988 was the first Presidential campaign ever where two candidates were clergymen: Pat Robertson and Jesse Jackson.

- Remarkably, in 1992 candidate Bill Clinton, a Baptist with an obvious affinity for religious language and themes,

    "carried three-fourths of the secular vote, while George H.W. Bush (41) won two-thirds of the traditionalists." (Phillips, quoting Bolce and de Maio, 189).

- The **religion gap** as measured by voting preference of "frequent attenders" rose from ten points in 1972 to fourteen in 1992 to **twenty points in 2000.**

Phillips explains the religion gap the same way that Islamists explain their anger at the United States: **it's the policies, stupid.** Even when Democrats put forward candidates who are arguably more religious than their Republican counterparts (compare Clinton with patrician G.H.W. Bush and sardonic Bob Dole), regular churchgoers are upset about Democratic policies on"abortion, gay marriage, ... prayer in schools." Again: **whose fault is that?** If your political faction puts forward a set of policies that demonstrably anger regular churchgoers—a slice of the population that for thousands of years has rightly been associated with law-abidingness and civic stability—**maybe your faction should rethink its policies.**

I THOROUGHLY ENJOYED PHILLIPS'S DISCUSSION OF THE 2004 ELECTION in the section titled *Born-Again Republicans: 2004 and the New Religiopolitical Map.* To begin with, he avoided some easy traps that have snared other commentators.

- I was thrilled that there was **no whining about vote fraud in Ohio.** The election is over, guys. **You lost.**

- I was also pleased to see that there was **no Kerry-bashing.** IIt's unfair to blame all the party's ills on him. **He came quite close to winning** the electoral vote. By any objective standard (applying no expectations or preconceptions) he did a reasonably good job at the task that was set before him; certainly far better than, say, Dukakis or McGovern; just not quite good enough.

- Phillips didn't fall into the trap of an abstract discussion about "values." I liked his crisp distinction that

```
"values are what society holds; what churches
    hold is theology and belief."
```

although I might quibble that neither society nor churches hold values, specific human individuals hold values.

PHILLIPS'S ANALYSIS OF THE ELECTION WAS, INDEED, MASTERLY. Bush's share of white evangelical Christians went from 72% in 2000 to 78% in 2004. **Red states** indeed! But it was not just about evangelicals. It was about policies tied to degree and nature of **religiosity.**

Bush picked up among Catholics, black protestants, and [Jews]. He increased his share of Jewish voters from 18.5% to approximately 25%, thanks in part to an 85% share among high-birth rate Orthodox and Haredi Jews. He increased from 8 percent to 11 percent among blacks, with a 22 percent share among black "frequent church attenders"; he says many black pastors emphasized the gay marriage issue. Conversely, Bush lost ground among American Muslims and "mainline" Protestants.

Phillips's Map 4 (199) of the Republican national coalition is very good; it's a shame he didn't have access to someone with real GIS tools to make the map in higher-resolution.

Figure 4, *The Theocratic Inclinations of the Republican Electorate,* could just as easily be titled *The Exaggerated Concerns of the Secular Analyst.* Once again, the poll questions do not pose critical tradeoffs. Are we supposed to be alarmed that 62% of Republicans answer "yes" to "Should a political leader rely on religion when making policy decisions?" I would be alarmed if the question read "Should a political leader rely *exclusively* on religion..." As posed, the question merely asks whether religion should be "part of the mix", and it is far more alarming, to my mind, that 65% of Democrats and 77% of Liberals say "no".

Similarly, it does not bother me that 62% of white conservative evangelicals believe that yes, "religious leaders [should] try to influence politicians' positions on the issues." **Freedom of speech, remember?** And the 71% of Democrats who answered "no" must have awfully short memories: what about the Reverend Martin Luther King? He did a pretty good job of influencing politicians' positions on the issues. **Good grief.**

As for the fact that 37% of Americans say "yes," religious leaders should try to influence government decisions, whereas only 12% of the French and 17% of Spaniards say "yes," well, it's no wonder: unlike France and Spain, America didn't have Cardinal Richelieu (the mustachio-twirling bad guy of the *Three Musketeer* movies) or **the Spanish Inquisition.** Phillips's normally acute sense of historical context deserts him at just the wrong moment!

We live in America, not France, not Spain; **we are entitled to the confidence in religious toleration that our history gives us.** We fought for it. We bled for it. We died for it. We paid for it. We prayed for it. It is ours. And it's time we started being proud of it.

Phillips is on safer ground when he discusses the difference between two-term Republican presidents Reagan and Bush. Figure 5 is an eye-opener, which shows that Bush's share of the total vote for President was between ten and twenty percent less in 2004 than Reagan's in 1984 in sixteen states. As Phillips observes, "we tend to forget how well Reagan did in this part of America." It's almost unimaginable to think about Bush or any Republican taking Massachusetts in 2008.

WHAT'S THE DIFFERENCE BETWEEN REAGAN AND DUBYA? Phillips doesn't really explain it, except to imply that Bush is sort of a successful version of Goldwater, a political fundamentalist aiming only at securing **"the base"** for an electoral majority. In another sense, though, Phillips argues that Bush is even dumber than Goldwater and Reagan: he won his (narrow) victory in part because he had a "politico-moral platform that neither Goldwater nor Reagan could have remotely contemplated": **9/11.**

IF YOU FIND THAT IDEA OFFENSIVE, you're not alone. Unfortunately, this is one of those annoying situations where about half the people think it's offensive to accuse Bush of politicizing 9/11, and about half the people think it's offensive that Bush did politicize 9/11. Phillips, obviously, is one of the latter category. He justifies this belief based on a set of "expert witnesses": **academic experts on religion.** Now *there's* a politically savvy, worldly wise group that's fully equipped to make subtle moral judgments about cause and effect in international politics. It's hard to imagine how Phillips could have come up with a more out-of-touch group of "experts" to explain the American reaction to 9/11.

PHILLIPS GETS SOME EXPERTS TO DEFINE FUNDAMENTALISM, then says fundamentalism sounds a lot like the Bush administration. Phillips quotes Charles Kimball identifying five "principal perverse fundamentalist" tendencies, but, to avoid the (accurate) perception of overreaching, Phillips hides the title of the Kimball book to an endnote: *When Religion Becomes Evil.* Then Phillips quotes Kimball saying that he had become "concerned" that the Bush administration met *two* of the five criteria for perverse fundamentalism. Case closed!?

The more overwhelming evidentiary objection to calling the Bush administration "fundamentalist" is to think for a moment about the people who actually have had the top jobs.

- Colin Powell
- Donald Rumsfeld
- Condi Rice
- Dick Cheney

- These are all people who have spent decades operating at the highest levels of government, academia, and politics. To me, these people look a lot more like political and bureaucratic operators than they look like fundamentalists. I would feel differently if the top policy jobs were held by people like:

- Billy Graham

- Pat Robertson

- James Falwell

Now, *those* are fundamentalists.

DOMKE, IN *GOD WILLING*, CARRIES OUT AN IMPRESSIVE TEXTUAL ANALYSIS, reviewing many of the speeches and public messages from the Bush administration. He concludes that the White House "marketed" (Phillips's word) or *"advocated"* (my word) a 'universal gospel of freedom and liberty' attributed to God. Basic question: **what's wrong with that?**

Well, of course, nothing is wrong with it, unless you **exaggerate and overreach.** Phillips quotes Domke: "Bush positions himself as a prophet, speaking for God." Look, let's get real. It's clear to me that George W. Bush is a religious person who believes that God sometimes speaks to him, like probably three quarters of the U.S. population. But does he think he is a prophet? No. **C'mon.** Everything we see about this man in public, he is a blunt-talking, competitive, sarcastic, practical man, who **doesn't look down at his feet and see sandals.**

PHILLIPS DROPS THE "T" BOMB at the beginning of the final section on *The Emerging Republican Theocracy.* He kicks off the section by redefining theocracy to fit his rhetoric: now it means

```
"some degree of rule by religion" (208).
```

Note the artfully palmed cards. "Some degree of rule by" is not the same as "rule by," which is what normal people mean when they say "plutocracy," "democracy", and "theocracy." And rule *"by religion"* is very different from rule by *religious leaders,* which again is what normal people mean when they think of "theocracies" like the Mullahs in Iran. Rule "by religion" is artfully vague because it means that rule is by a huge, extremely diverse conceptual entity, not by specific people.

A MULTIPLE-CHOICE QUIZ asks whether "theocracy" in the U.S. boils down to A) a legitimate fear B) a joke given the hugely secular American"culture" or C) a worrisome tendency of conservatives or D) all of the above. Phillips's answer is D) which seems somewhat unfair given that two out of the three answers are hostile to theocracy.

A PUTATIVELY HYPOTHETICAL SCENARIO for "incipient theocracy" looks just like the worst religio-political excesses of the present day. **Scary!** Then Phillips quotes the following sources to back up his no-longer-hypothetical conclusion:

- Pollsters
- Activists on both sides
- Europeans (I'm not kidding!)

The reliance on European experts is especially hilarious, as Phillips rolls out Jacques Delors, the former president of the European Commission, to opine that "the clash between those who believe and those who don't believe will be a dominant aspect of relations [between the United States and Europe] in the coming years." Well, not when you're **burning in Hell** it won't, you surrender-eating cheese monkey! Seriously, the idea that religious Americans are going to waste even a moment worrying about European views on religion just shows how irrelevant the Eurocrats are.

To be fair, some Europeans have reason to hate religion, as Phillips quotes (another Frenchman) Dominique Moisi: "We feel betrayed by God and by nationalism, which is why we are building the European Union as a barrier to religious warfare." Oh, I thought you were building it to prevent more wars like World War Two, **which wasn't about religion at all,** and to make Europe a counterpoise to American (and Chinese!) power.

Dr. Moisi is senior adviser to the French Institute of International Affairs; chief editor of Politique Etrangère, the Institute's quarterly publication; and a professor at the Institute of Political Studies in Paris. His advice is brought to you by Kevin Phillips, master of the authoritative quote from the self-interested authority.

THE DEFINITION OF CHUTZPAH is the man who kills his parents, then asks the court for mercy because he's an orphan. Once again, Phillips demonstrates that he has a mild to moderate case of chutzpah, as he recites a laundry list of (effective) Republican efforts to mobilize religious voters in 2004 and 2005(not mentioning any ineffective Democratic efforts to do the same thing), then undercuts his own argument by admitting that "this stops short of a merger of church and state."(213)

THE ASSEMBLIES OF GOD, MORMONS, AND LUTHERANS ARE UNCLE TOMS, Phillips seems to be saying (the offensive phrase is mine, not his), with a lamentable history of "accommodating state power." **It's not their fault, exactly:** the very fact that they are pre-eminent in particular regions of the country tends to breed "a powerful clerical closeness to everyday community governance and political authority." But as far as Phillips is concerned, that geographic concentration is bad news: it's like **a building block for theocracy.**

I FIND IT CURIOUS that Phillips does not discuss the geographic concentration of African-American churchgoers in major urban areas. Why doesn't *that* tend to breed a "powerful clerical closeness to ... political authority"? Oh, wait: **it does.** I live near Detroit, a city where it is pretty much impossible to be Mayor without strong endorsements from the leading black churches. Many other American cities exhibit similar patterns of threatening alignment between churches and predominantly Democratic office-holders. Why aren't **black Democratic theocrats** part of the discussion here?

If **Jesse Jackson** had his way, the black religious community would be just as effective as the Christian Coalition. You can bet that if black major-city pastors had their way, the Democratic party would be one heck of a lot more "theocratically" inclined. If **Democratic theocrats are irrelevant**, that is measure, perhaps, of their smaller absolute number, and, perhaps, of the failure of the liberal community to forge a successful alliance with people of faith.

THE MOST ENTERTAINING PORTION of this final section is a series of terrifying pull quotes from religious right leaders "letting the mask slip," in Phillips's words, about their desire **to run everything.**

- Jerry Falwell wants to eliminate public schools.

- **Pat Robertson** wants to **tear down that wall** of separation between church and state.

- The Reverend Sun Myung Moon (!!) believes "we must have an autocratic theocracy to run the world."

- **Pat Robertso**n wants to run government **according "to the laws of Jacob."** (Why not Jesus? Or Moses?)

I'm quaking in my boots.

Phillips's idea that this collection of bozos is representative of evangelical Christianity is **a real hoot.** I ask myself what the members of my southern Michigan Christian & Missionary Alliance church would make of the Reverend Moon's comment. I'd be laughed out of the room.

To be fair, there are quite a few people in the church who send their kids to private religious schools, and I know a couple who would be happy to run government according to Mosaic law. But the idea that these upper-middle-class **burghers**, as a group, want to exercise theocratic control over the local public schools is simply a non-starter: our community, Saline, just built an $89 million, 500,000 square foot, **Taj Mahal** of a public high school.[31] It is the key engine for giving their children a future. People in the congregation would be happy if prayer were allowed in the local schools, and if the curriculum was a bit more friendly to our Judeo-Christian history, but these parents would move out of town **in a heartbeat** if anything happened to bring down the reputation of Saline's public schools for high-quality education.

CATHOLIC SCHOOLS USED TO HAVE THAT REPUTATION, but Catholic schools aren't what they used to be. For that matter, neither are Catholics. Phillips documents without really discussing that many Catholics in America have become **among the wimpiest of all church-goers**, with only 32 percent of Catholics claiming that their personal religious views and faith influenced their voting patterns.

Did the decline in Catholic religiosity hurt the Democratic party? My intuition is that it did: Democrats lost the Archie Bunker vote about the same time Archie stopped believing.

Does the waning of Catholic religiosity work for or against theocracy? My intuition is that it works against the thesis of Phillips's book, in that there are at last count 62 million Catholics in America (Noll, 2000) w**ho are heading for the exit doors from theocracy** as fast as they can.

ARE 100 PERCENT APPROVAL RATINGS FROM THE CHRISTIAN COALITION among seven of the top Republican leaders in the

---

[31] http://www.salineschools.com/newhighschoolfacts.html

United States Senate a sign of impending theocracy? Phillips thinks so (216); I do have to admit **I would be happier if a few of them scored 60s or 80s.** I must note, though, that there is considerable irony in Phillips's quotation of the well regarded Representative Chris Shays of Connecticut (Phillips's home state) 2005 comment that "the Republican Party of Lincoln has become a party of theocracy."

IF EVER THERE WAS A GOD-BREATHED POLITICIAN IN UNITED STATES HISTORY, surely it was Abraham Lincoln. Where does Chris Shays think Lincoln got his religious faith? Where does he think he would get it today? Whatever we were doing back in those days to produce men with faith like Lincoln's, **maybe we should do a bit more of it today.** Phillips thinks believers want their government "to come from religious institutions"; maybe what believers want is simply to strengthen the churches that produce Bible-reading, God-fearing saints like Abraham Lincoln.

WORST THREAT TO SCIENCE SINCE GALILEO? That's what "some commentators" (not listed in the endnotes!) think all this theocracy is leading to.

EVEN WORSE, APPARENTLY, is the possibility that all this religious know-nothingism is going to lead to the United States's decline as a world economic power. The historical precedents for that possibility are the subject of the next chapter. But first I have to ask:

Who cares, really? Who really suffers when a country loses its "great power" status?

I was glad to see that self-styled "Sixties activist" Edward Jayne shared my skepticism on this score.

> We seem stymied in the sixtieth year of our
> hegemonic fling, half the period of time enjoyed
> by England. Like Germany, which consumed itself in
> the seven decades that elapsed between the Franco-

Prussian War and Hitler's defeat, our claim to imperial status seems in trouble almost before it began, and without the many cultural benefits that both England and Germany enjoyed during their heyday -- their science, philosophy, literature, music and art. Like Spain during the sixteenth and seventeenth centuries, we have little to show for our successes. Spain invented Don Quixote; we've invented electronic technology and the atomic bomb.

Does this mean that the Iraq debacle predicts utter collapse for the United States? Not at all. One suspects a "soft landing" will happen instead. Bush or one of his successors in the White House will find a respectable way to remove the American presence from Iraq, and our political and economic leadership will do everything necessary to maneuver a gentle aftermath when the dollar finally bottoms out, as it shall. Afterwards we will be able to carry on with our lives just as Spaniards have done since the seventeenth century, just as the French have done since Waterloo, and just as the English and Germans have done since the end of World War II. And, lest we forget, just as Canada has done since its very beginning. Of course our imperial pretensions will be far more modest than before, but we shall be better for it. And eventually we might live down our infamous reputation acquired in both Vietnam and Iraq.[32]

---

[32] Edward Jayne, "Bush Does Iraq: Anatomy of a Failed Operation" http://www.dissidentvoice.org/July06/Jayne20.htm

It seems to me that ordinary people in Spain, the Netherlands, and the United Kingdom enjoy pretty decent lives today. One could argue that the poor suffer, because they lose the opportunity to escape out of poverty, or the middle classes who see their lucrative industrial jobs replaced by humiliating service sector jobs; but I personally believe that it's **the elites who have the most at stake.** All of a sudden, you go from complaining about the course of the world's most important country to complaining about the course of the world's tenth or twentieth most important country. You go from being a medium sized fish in a big pond to being a medium sized fish in a medium sized pond. It's quite a comedown.

ADVANCING THE DEBATE: When we talk about religious people mixing in politics, we need to keep these things in mind:

1. What matters to some people is whether they are **walking the path of righteousness.** The concept of righteousness is as old as human history, and it is not going away. It is pointless to try to exclude it.

2. Democrats need to start figuring out **how their party is going to support religion in the United States.** If they can't do that, they're never going to get themselves out of the hole they have dug themselves in **the most religious country in the industrialized world.**

Church, State, and National Decline

SMART-ALEC SUMMARY: K-Phil sez: We're going the way of Spain, the Netherlands, and Great Britain. America sez: **Who?**

EPIGRAPH #1: A RE-RUN OF THE BILL MOYERS QUOTE that "the delusional is no longer marginal." As I said the first time Phillips used this quote, I don't think that's anything new.

EPIGRAPH #2: IF *THE ECONOMIST* SAYS IT, IT MUST BE TRUE. Even if the Economist is just reporting that "liberals" think between a quarter and a third of the population is bent on creating a theocracy.

EPIGRAPH #3: FINALLY, A CREDIBLE SOURCE! FORMER SENATOR JOHN DANFORTH saying that "Republicans have transformed our party into the political arm of conservative Christians." It's interesting to note where Danforth assigns the responsibility for action: with Republicans, not with Christians.

PHILLIPS STARTS OFF WELL IN THIS CHAPTER with the sensible observation that Americans, faced with a broad range of diverse threats in the early 2000s, made many different choices about which threats to emphasize. I found myself nodding in agreement as Phillips pointed out that while "conservatives saw a threat that was predominantly religious and moral ... among secular voters a startling two-thirds expressed antipathy to evangelicals." This image of fingers pointing at each other encapsulates a lot of American politics today.

Unfortunately, **Phillips lost me** when he tried to zoom out to emphasize his own **pet threat:** "the precedents of past leading world economic powers show that blind faith and religious excesses ... have often contributed to national decline..." I simply don't accept that losing our status as a world economic power is the most important threat facing us today. **What's the worst that could happen?**

GDP growth could slow down. Big deal! Average life expectancy in Great Britain actually increased from 69 in 1955 (when it lost its stature as a great power) to 78 in 2002.[33]

Later in this chapter, Phillips himself identifies a threat that I would regard as far more significant: the threat of a future Disenlightenment, or *The Closing of the Western Mind,* in the words of Charles A. Freeman's book. I got chills when I read the passage Phillips quotes from Freeman to the effect that there was **a gap of more than thousand years** between the last astronomical observation in 475 A.D. and the publication of Copernicus's *De Revolutionibus* in 1543. But whereas the Dark Ages affected all of Europe, and the shutdown of learning was nearly complete, no such complete threat looms for America. We are embedded in a global system of science and technology that is not going away, despite the Unabomber's most vicious attacks. The worst that could happen is that we will no longer be the leader in science in technology. That would be bad, but exactly how bad would it be?

I would submit that there is, in fact, a very real and very specific threat that we should be far more concerned about, and which, in fact, is the primary concern of the much-maligned Bush Administration: namely, the use of w**eapons of mass destruction** against the United States. This threat is different from all others – moral decline, global warming, intolerance, HIV, Disenlightenment, theocracy – because it involves the possible

---

[33] "Is Capitalism Good for the Poor?" by professor Gary Walton ofor the Foundation for Teaching Economics, http://www.fte.org/capitalism/introductiono2.php

immediate, near-term death of millions of people and the permanent crippling of the United States.

The winning move for the enemy in the current "war" is **the simultaneous explosion of three or more untraceable nuclear devices in major cities of the United States.** My assessment is that such a decapitation strike would create such crushing humanitarian and financial burden that the United States simply would never be able to recover. This scenario is by no means an impossibility. If terrorists can get their hands on one nuclear device, why not three or five? And the "state of the art" for terror is multiple simultaneous strikes with maximum impact.

I will say more about this scenario in a future book, but for the moment I wish simply to note that, in my view, Kevin Phillips doesn't have his eye on the ball. The things he's worried about simply aren't that important, or that fatal, compared to the real threat that is before us.

I should add that my logic applies to cultural conservatives as well: Disenlightenment is a folly we can't afford when our survival as a nation may depend on our technical ability to detect weapons of mass destruction before they are used. I would not go so far as to say that spiritual matters pale before survival, but I would say that if we are tested by a decapitation strike, the church in the United States will have to be both stronger *and* smarter than it ever has before. There can be no descent into medievalism when the survival of the society itself may be at stake.

EXCESSIVE RELIGIOSITY LEADS TO NATIONAL DECLINE, according to Phillips, and he thinks **he knows it when he sees it.** (Excessive and harmful religiosity, that is.) The first half of this chapter is devoted to exploring five "critical symptoms of decline."

Table 3. Symptoms of national decline

What Phillips says	What he means
"[W]idespread public concern over cultural and economic decay…"	Whining.
"Growing religious fervor…"	Pushy preachers.
"Rising commitment to faith … downplaying of science."	Blue-state know-nothings who don't know their place.
"… [P]opular anticipation of … an epochal battle…"	Kooks.
"National strategic … overreach…"	Iraq.

Phillips finds all these symptoms in his sample of four (4) previous leading world economic and military powers:

- Rome
- Spain
- Netherlands
- Great Britain

DOESN'T THIS LIST SEEM A BIT EUROCENTRIC TO YOU? It's obvious that Phillips's history education predates the great "diversity" wave that swept through American higher education leaving most American students with a random assortment of factoids about "other cultures" and an even sketchier knowledge of their own history.

Left unsaid: the possibility that America might be following another imperial model. What if it turns out that America, as a culturally homogenous, highly meritocratic, continental power, is more like the Chinese Empire than the Roman? Then we would be looking at a three thousand year run with periodic ups and downs. That's a considerably more optimistic metaphor!

MERCIFULLY, PHILLIPS DISCUSSES ROME AND THE EMPEROR CONSTANTINE without mentioning *The Da Vinci Code*.

THE KINGS OF SPAIN WERE A BUNCH OF SUCKERS, as far as Phillips is concerned, because they lived up to their vows to support the Catholic church. He is not impressed by the idea that "the Catholic identity was Spain's greatest legacy" (222) or by Phillip II's vow that "rather than suffer the least damage to the Catholic Church and God's service, I will lose all my states and a hundred lives if I had them." Phillips dryly comments,

> "What Spain did lose was worldly power and hegemony." (223)

As a committed Christian, I have no difficulty in imagining that a reasonable person might consider the spiritual welfare of millions of souls more important than worldly power and hegemony.

THE DUTCH NEVER MADE A COMEBACK TO THEIR GLORY YEARS of the 17th Century, and Phillips blames "the divisive legacy of early Dutch religious zealotry." To this observer, it seems that the Netherlands's small size relative to France and Great Britain probably had a lot to do with it too.

PHILLIPS IS IN HIS ELEMENT as he discusses the muscular evangelism of Victorian Great Britain.

> "Moral pretension became a second British flag, just as it later became a second American flag."

Really? Of course, it's easy to construct an argument that British and American foreign policies have been hypocritical, power-hungry, and unjust in dozens of countries on hundreds of occasions in the last two centuries at a horrible cost in lives and justice. But before we take it as a given that Great Britain and America are pretentious moral hypocrites, let's remember the hundreds of millions of immigrants to both countries over the last two centuries who have **voted with their feet.** There's a parallel reality that must be accounted for; a *genuine* moral claim, staked by the Magna Carta and the U.S. Constitution, backed by our contributions to the defeat of a succession of tyrant—including Napoleon, the Kaiser, Hitler, Stalin, and Brezhnev—who killed and enslaved hundreds of millions of people.

THE PLAYING FIELDS OF ETON WERE NOT PAVED WITH BUNSEN BURNERS, and Phillips attributes some of the British elite's antipathy to science to the pernicious influence of religiosity.

ROMAN DECAY IS A CLICHÉ – Nero lolling on his sofa eating grapes – and Phillips rightly notes that Romans were very concerned about it. What strikes me is that they were concerned about it for **a very long time.** Four hundred years (give or take) is a long time for an empire to be in decline. That's a lot of human lives who were still part of the empire when it was an empire. At the moment, it seems quite unlikely that the United States will maintain its hegemony for anywhere near four hundred years (dating from 1945). On the other hand, if you look strictly at the number of years, our hegemony has only lasted sixty years so far; Rome, Spain, and Britain all had considerably longer runs. If the United States hegemony lasts, say, fifty more years, **it will outlive Kevin Phillips and most of his readers.** That's an awful lot like Phillips being **wrong.**

THE PARADOX OF AMERICAN OVERREACH is that just when it seemed most plausible to argue that we were overstretched, we won the Cold War, freeing up all those overstretched resources. Whoops!

Now people are arguing that we're overstretched again. A lot of otherwise sensible people like Thomas Barnett (*Pentagon's New Map*) think our 140,000 troops in Iraq mean we're "pinned down" there. I'm not so sure. I think that if push comes to shove, the

United States still has a lot of "surge capability" to deal with other threats.

Phillips wisely confines himself to raising the reasonable question whether events in the 21st century may "punish American overstretch."

(Some might say that the answer is a "**slam dunk**", in the memorable phrase attributed to George Tenet as he assured President Bush that there were weapons of mass destruction in Iraq.)

SUMMING UP this trip through Phillips's brief history of imperial decline, current day America meets most or all of Phillips's criteria, and he wants us to be worried: **very, very worried.**

IN THE NEXT SECTION, *A Twenty-First-Century American Disenlightenment,* we learn that Phillips thinks **John Ashcroft is a loon.**

We also learn that Phillips unquestioningly accepted Ron Suskind's famous sound-bite from an unnamed Republican disparaging the "reality-based community." **Anyone who <u>ever</u> mentions the "reality-based community" should also read Mickey Kaus's classic demolition** in *Slate* on October 26, 2004

> The problem with this now-famous anecdote is that it has **nothing to do with certainty based on religious faith** or with the tension "between fact and faith" that Suskind claims to find in the Bush White House. The aide isn't talking about ignoring reality and living in some spiritual dream world, he's talking about *changing* reality through worldly action (e.g. war). His point is less Christian than Marxist, a vulgar Bush corrolary to Marx's famous *Theses on Feuerbach,* the last of which is carved into his tombstone: "The

philosophers have only *interpreted* the world, in
various ways; the point, however, is to *change*
it." The press and much of Washington *studies* the
existing world in various ways, the "senior
advisor" seems to be saying. "Meanwhile we're
changing the world in ways that make your studies
obsolete."

As a macho pledge to create new facts on the
ground, this boast may be arrogant (there are
obvious Sharonist overtones). As a commentary on
the reification at the core of the Washington
world view--on the tendency of "many ... elected
officials" to assume that the way the world is is
the way it will stay and must stay--there's a
certain amount of revolutionary wisdom in it. But
it ain't about religion. The faith it exhibits
isn't a faith in a higher power but faith in
earthly political power. (I'd say it was
Nietzschian, if I knew what that meant!)

If Suskind misreads his own facts wrong in
order to (willfully? subconsciously?) pander to
New York Times readers' fear of Christian
fundamentalism, what other facts has he misread?
And what kind of 'empiricist' is he?[34]

It is exactly this sort of critical thinking that Phillips needs to apply
to his own sources more frequently.

THEOLOGICAL CORRECTNESS, a phrase introduced in this section, is
a useful way to capture the painful stupidity that sometimes ensues
when "litmus test" religious thinking is applied in an uncritical way,
but I find myself saddened by the phrase, too.   We talk

---

[34] http://www.slate.com/id/2108682/

disparagingly about politics, and political correctness, but, properly understood, **theology**, like politics, philosophy, and mathematics, is **a profound and noble discipline** that is at the heart of the human experience. I wish there was more theology in this book about theocracy.

PHILLIPS HAS A PERFECT OPPORTUNITY to engage with the substance of theology in the next section, *The Theologization of American Politics: Symptoms and Prescriptions,* and I was glad to see that he does lay out some reasonable views, but he often slips into easy caricatures. Let me mention a few of the more egregious howlers.

"IN THE BIBLE, DEATH COMES LIGHTLY," Phillips opines, after reviewing a study by Donald Akenson counting up the number of dead in the BibleNow, anyone who has ever flipped through the Old Testament knows that there is a grain of truth in this assessment; but anyone who has ever read and pondered on the Bible at any length also knows that there's quite a bit of stuff in there about **respect for life.** (Many Christians like to talk about the Bible as **God's love letter to humanity.**)

"OVERALL THEOLOGY ACCORDS WOMEN SECONDARY STATUS," according to Phillips, "within the Republican party's most loyal denominations"—Southern Baptists, Mormons, and Missouri Synod Lutherans, Again, as anyone who has ever set foot in a church knows, there's a grain of truth, but Phillips's sweeping summation is not exactly the whole truth and nothing but the truth. For one thing, women play a key role in most American churches, often far outpacing men in their visible devotion and involvement. Baptist churches without women would be pretty puny things. For another thing, the famous New Testament verses that describe the man as the head of the family also emphasize that he is to be a servant to his wife.

Wives, submit to your husbands as to the Lord.
For the husband is the head of the wife as Christ

126

is the head of the church, his body, of which he
is the Savior. Now as the church submits to
Christ, so also wives should submit to their
husbands in everything.

Husbands, love your wives, just as Christ
loved the church and gave himself up for her to
make her holy, cleansing[a] her by the washing with
water through the word, and to present her to
himself as a radiant church, without stain or
wrinkle or any other blemish, but holy and
blameless. In this same way, husbands ought to
love their wives as their own bodies. He who loves
his wife loves himself. After all, no one ever
hated his own body, but he feeds and cares for it,
just as Christ does the church— for we are members
of his body. "For this reason a man will leave his
father and mother and be united to his wife, and
the two will become one flesh."[b] This is a
profound mystery—but I am talking about Christ and
the church. However, each one of you also must
love his wife as he loves himself, and the wife
must respect her husband. (Ephesians 5:21-32, NIV)

While this is not entirely a 21st-century view of the relationship
between man and woman, neither is it a rallying cry for misogyny.

LOOKING BACK AT IT, JOE MCCARTHY WAS RIGHT, Phillips suggests
in a rather bizarre allusion to the "release in recent decades of old
Soviet files ... [that] confirmed some of what [1940's and 1950's]
conservatives were charging ... [about fellow travelers]" (245).
Therefore, "today's liberal and progressive muckrakers are
probably just as accurate in suggesting a larger-than-realized
influence of Christian Reconstructionists" (bogeymen who believe
in "reconstructing" current American society to be ready for the
imminent advent of Jesus Christ). The logic here is so tenuous it's

hard to know where to start deconstructing it. Conservatives were right sixty years ago, so liberals are probably right today?

CHRISTIAN RECONSTRUCTIONISM is a big Phillips bogeyman; the fear-mongering is made easier by his comment that not many people identify openly as Christian Reconstructionists. In fact, it may also be the case that not many people, numerically speaking, are interested in this particular concept. Look at this Google Trends graph, comparing the number of searches on "theocracy" and "reconstructionism."

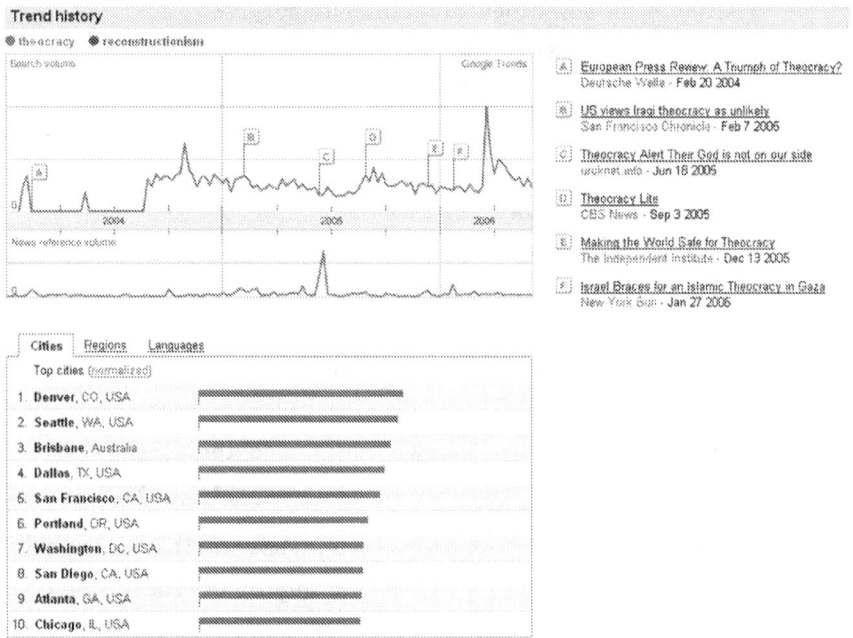

Figure 8. Theocracy v. Reconstructionism

The search trend on "theocracy" shows a big upward spike at the time of release of *American Theocracy*.

There is no search trend data for "reconstructionism," meaning that very few people in the Google sample are using the term.

According to Phillips, "the groups that monitor such activists ... take the movement ... seriously." Well, of course they do.

Question: if a group's members have never heard of it, just how much of a threat can it be?

Phillips jumps from asserting that Christian Reconstructionism is an important movement to asserting that it has a strong influence on the Southern Baptist Convention and other evangelical organizations. He may not necessarily be wrong, but he hasn't done a very good job of proving his case.

IN 2005, JAMES DOBSON POINTED OUT that Congress created the 9th Circuit of Appeals and could, if it wished, uncreate it. From my understanding of constitutional law (I got an "A" in the course in law school, but that's about it) this is a true statement, although un-creating a Federal appeals court would not be a swift process— all the parties before that court would need to get due process as their cases were migrated to other appeals courts. But Phillips thinks we should get upset that the idea was even put on the table. **Why?** As a practical matter, it is very unlikely, to put it mildly, that Congress will ever disenfranchise the 9th Circuit of Appeals. Again, let's worry about actual problems, not bogeymen.

AMERICAN TEENAGERS ARE DUMB, according to Phillips, citing well-known figures about science and math scores for high schoolers (248), but failing to mention countervailing positive statistics about this country's great proficiency at training its young people in the "soft skills" needed for entrepreneurship. America's well known educational problems are what social scientists call **"overdetermined"**: there are dozens of social factors that contribute to the problems and it hardly seems fair to blame religion for them, especially when some of the factors are completely secular in nature (television) and some of them are arguably solved by *more* religion (materialistic, stressed, fragmented families).

PHILLIPS TURNS SOME NICE PHRASES in this section. For example, I liked his offhand reference to "**the next throbbing cluster of issues**" involving church-state relations.

PHILLIPS ALSO HAS A KEEN EYE FOR DETAIL (*too* keen for his own good, maybe)! I was intrigued by a couple of paragraphs on the "Name It and Claim It" theology which some Christians use to excuse a self-centered focus on material success. It's fascinating stuff, and it certainly helps explain the co-existence of intense religiosity and mass materialism, but it doesn't have much to do with the Bible, as anyone who has read the New Testament realizes. Yes, Jesus was a carpenter—**one of the "tech geeks" of his time, as** I hope to explain in a future book—but his journey to the cross was all about giving up material wealth.

CHRISTIANS HAVE BEEN GETTING THINGS CONFUSED FOR CENTURIES, starting with Jesus and going on through **the Crusades** to the Inquisition to the present day, so it's not entirely unfair for Phillips to skewer materialistic Christians. Similarly, the concluding section of this chapter rests on Phillips's argument that present day Americans are confusing the war against Islam in the modern era with **the Crusades.** Again, this is not an unreasonable argument, as the last few years have seen our President repeatedly use the word "crusade" to describe what would be more effectively referred to as **GSAVE, the "global struggle against violent extremism"**, and conservative columnist Ann Coulter suggest, shortly after 9/11, that we should "invade their countries, kill their leaders, and convert them to Christianity." Phillips does a nice job of walking us through the historical precedents of great empires where religious fervor has fueled expansionist fires. As usual, though, the force of Phillips's argument is greatly weakened when we make an effort to remember all the ways in which the present-day USA is different from medieval Crusaders or British imperial evangelists. To name only a few key differences:

This is 2006, not 1206. The current human population of the USA is vastly more numerous, healthier, and better educated than the population of medieval Europe. We're not looking at a crusade to Damascus as a superior alternative to **battling off rats in the gutters of London.**

The United States is arguably both the most religiously diverse and the most religiously tolerant nation in world history.

The intense religiosity of the United States is embedded within an equally intense secular **frenzy of capitalism, globalization, science, technology, and materialism,** in all of which the notion of a religiously motivated Crusade is absurd.

The political entity known as the United States of America is formally organized as a presidential republic, not as an empire. Indeed, the United States Constitution explicitly forbids officers of the United States government from holding monarchical titles.

Time's arrow runs in one direction only. Simply put, 2006 is *after* 1206 and it is *after* 1906. We have already been through the Crusades and we have already been through the First World War and the fall of Britain's global empire. Although there is certainly plenty of reason to be cynical about the human tendency to repeat mistakes, we have already "been there, done that," with the Crusades and Victorian Imperialism. My view is that George Santayana has been superseded by Henry Ford: although "those who forget history may be condemned to repeat it,"{check quote} the history of the 21st Century is more likely to be, in Ford's words, "one damn thing after another": a string of *new* blunders and catastrophes that feel not so much cyclical as random.

With these major points of perspective established, let's take a quick walk through Phillips's argument that we are embarked on a new Crusade.

AFTER BLAMING THE BELLICOSITY OF BRITAIN'S CHURCHES for World War I, Phillips swiftly pivots U.S. churches needed a replacement target for the evil empire that was the former Soviet Union and quickly settled on Islam, Iraq, and Saddam Hussein as the stand-ins for the forces of evil, Babylon, and the anti-Christ respectively.

PHILLIPS THEN BLAMES *AMERICAN* CHURCHES for not "inoculating" themselves against dangerous *Left Behind* theology with a more sensible brand of eschatology. The result, he implies, will be a 21st-Century catastrophe that may do to American religion what the Great War did to English religion. Once again, remember that these two things are different. We haven't yet had a 21st-Century catastrophe that is anywhere close to as much of a global disaster as the First World War, and there are good reasons to think that we won't—the existence of nuclear weapons has created a barrier to full-out war that may never be crossed again. Moreover, the America of 2006, the world's most religiously diverse and religiously tolerant nation, which has a clause in its Constitution prohibiting the establishment of a state religion, is very different from the relatively homogenous England of 1914 and its Anglican church.

MODERN AMERICA AND IMPERIAL GREAT BRITAIN have both found themselves in conflict with Islam. Is that our fault, or Islam's fault? Then as now, the countries of the Islamic crescent have been managed by corrupt, inefficient governments and dominated by real religious theocracies.

RELIGIOUS BUSH-BACKERS ARE STUPID, Phillips concludes, on the basis of polling data in 2004 that found three-quarters of Bush backers still convinced that Iraq had WMD and was aiding al-Qaeda. Not just foolishly stupid, for tolerating "cognitive dissonance," but dangerously stupid, because they have the United States in the grip of their "powerful religiosity ... and biblical worldview."

IT SHOULD BE OBVIOUS, BUT APPARENTLY ISN'T, that explaining a disagreement by saying "the other guys are stupid" isn't a tremendously constructive approach.

ADVANCING THE DEBATE: At this point in the book, I think the most valuable thing I can do to advance the debate about the role of evangelism in American politics and American foreign policy is to tell you a little story about the professor who taught the American Foreign Policy seminar at Swarthmore College in the fall of 1981.

Professor James Kurth was a brilliant and engaging teacher, but there was something about him that frightened me, and throughout the time I knew him my dominant attitude was one of profound wariness. While his expressed political views were always articulated in a logical and eminently defensible form, I suspected him of being a secret bomb-thrower; a cynic and anarchist at heart who would be among the first comrades lopping off my bourgeois head come the Revolution.

I had already taken a Defense Policy course from him in fall 1980 (if I remember the date correctly). In that course, I got an A, which I expected given my lifelong fascination with military history. The most memorable thing that occurred in that first interaction with Kurth was that a few weeks into the course I wrote a letter to the editor of the college newspaper, The Phoenix, pointing out that there was not a single woman in the class of twenty-plus students. The letter stirred up some interest and a woman joined the class. Looking back, I think Kurth must have been happy about the letter.

In the spring of 1981 Kurth picked me to go to a workshop at the U.S. Naval Academy. I was supposed to write a five-page paper and participate in some sort of exercise—the details are fuzzy. What I do remember is that I didn't write the paper, and, although I set out by train for Annapolis, I never made it there. Instead I wound up at a phone booth somewhere near Washington, D.C., asking my grandmother Zimmerman to let me stay overnight at her house in

Alexandria and pay my train fare back to Swarthmore. I remember that I procrastinated about the paper, then was too embarrassed to go to the workshop –but I don't remember why I left campus, or what the thought processes were that led me to being stranded and out of cash in a major urban center. You might think drugs or alcohol were involved, but, no; I simply had some major problems with depression and irresponsibility in those days.

Later that same spring I decided to write a senior thesis, and since the topic pertained to American foreign policy, Kurth's subject, asked Kurth if he would be my thesis adviser. I was surprised and hurt when he said no. He said something to the effect that "I don't think our temperaments are compatible." I didn't know what he meant, but thought that he might be saying he thought I was too conservative for him.

Looking back, I can hardly wonder that he turned me down, but I do wish he had been more explicit about his reasons. I was badly in need of a wake up call, and I think I might have responded well to a stern message to the effect that he would be my adviser only if I made a commitment to be a hell of a lot more responsible going forward.

I recovered my balance pretty well—simply asked another professor to be my adviser and went forward with the thesis. I didn't have enough initiative in those days to do the archival research that would have made the thesis outstanding, so it wound up being merely passable. I went ahead and took the double-credit American Foreign Policy seminar from Kurth, and enjoyed it a lot. He was an excellent teacher. But he still gave me a feeling of danger, and I didn't trust him.

I graduated from Swarthmore in the spring of 1982 and went to work as writer for a personal computer magazine. A few years after I married Cheryl in 1989, I began going to evangelical churches in Michigan and Ohio, and my faith grew steadily. I didn't pay much attention to American foreign policy in the next twenty years, and Professor Kurth slipped out of my mind.

I came across him again while doing research for *American Theocracy Unpacked*, when I found a fascinating interview with him on the web site Beliefnet.[35] The interviewer, Alice Chasan, titled the interview "Debunking *American Theocracy*" and summarized it this way:

> The Bush administration isn't too Christian,
> says politics professor James Kurth--it's not
> Christian enough.

My favorite passage from this interview was this:

> In all of his account of evangelicals in his
> book, Phillips almost never quotes any
> conversation he had with an actual living,
> breathing evangelical. He refers to the famous
> novels in the "Left Behind" series, or to this or
> that statement by this or that purported
> representative of evangelicals, often whom are
> simply paid lobbyists in Washington, or perhaps
> politicians. But, he almost never talks to and
> listens to evangelicals out there in the America
> that he's talking about.
>
> I have talked to such evangelicals, and I
> arrive at a very different conception of their
> understanding of end times than Phillips does. And
> I can delineate some of those differences. First,
> it is true that evangelicals, especially those
> believing in biblical inerrancy, will of course
> take the Book of Revelation to be inerrant, and

_____

[35] http://www.beliefnet.com/story/192/story_19276_1.html

that in the fullness of time there will be the end times as described in the Book of Revelation.

But of course, and not only in the Book of Revelation, but in other books of the New Testament as well, it is made crystal clear that no man knows the time of the coming of Jesus, the Messiah. We are not to know that.

In addition, however, we are to live as if it could happen tomorrow. And we are also to live as if no one knows when it will come. Therefore, we must be simultaneously prepared for it to come tomorrow, or indeed in the next instant, or to not come for generations. And it is presumptuous for any person to claim it's coming any day now or in our own lifetime. That is another form of heresy, of false prophecy.

That is what Bible-believing evangelicals believe. They have a humility about their knowledge of the end times. And they must pick up the burden of being ready simultaneously to receive the coming of the Lord and to still be in the world but not of it, working to carry out the Lord's will.

So, when Phillips says evangelicals are anticipating the end times coming very shortly, and this, therefore, determines their policy on such a wide range of things as the environment and the Middle East, and attitudes toward social or environmental problems, this is simply a falsehood about the understanding of the vast bulk of evangelicals. They assume the end times will come, but they in turn are still given the call for good

stewardship, to tend the garden of the world, to
be peacemakers.

Exactly.

> On one of my leaves, when I was teaching at UC
> at San Diego, a student asked me if I read the
> Bible. So I kind of sloughed him off and said
> something like "oh sure, every once in a while."
> He immediately said "what's your favorite book?" I
> was going through some physical challenges at the
> time so I said "oh, I don't know, maybe the Book
> of Job." "That's great," he said. "We're having a
> Bible study meeting on Wednesday and that's the
> book we're going to talk about." I said �oh, I
> already have a commitment this Wednesday, I can't
> go." "How about next week?" And he had me. I was
> stuck. So I went. And I was impressed. There were
> then a series of events, a cascade of experiences,
> that I now consider to be the work of the Holy
> Spirit or divine intervention, that led me closer
> to the church and to faith. And I was "on line" as
> of March 1980. I'm still in touch with that
> student and his family and am something of an
> uncle to their seven children.

Kurth, like me, has little difficulty in finding examples of Phillips's
tendency for sloppiness and exaggeration.[36]/

> There is also no evidence whatever that he read
> what he purports to be an extremely important and
> dangerous book that, according to Phillips, shaped
> President Bush's views of dealing with Iraq. That
> book is Oswald Chambers' book of devotions, whose

---

[36] http://www.swarthmore.edu/news/kurth/

title which Phillips does not give, "My Utmost for His Highest."

Phillips points out that Oswald Chambers was a preacher to the British forces stationed in Egypt in 1917 in the First World War, on the eve of going into Palestine and into Iraq. And he leaves the impression that this book was essentially a rallying of the British troops to carry a crusade into Palestine and to Iraq. And he, therefore, leaves the impression that when Bush was reading this book prior to the invasion of Iraq that that was--he was also being inspired by this evangelical Bible-believing Christian to a crusade.

Well, I happen to have read that book...

Shades of Lloyd Bentsen demolishing Dan Quayle!

... It is a book of daily devotions. There is a one page entry for every day of the year. There is no reference whatever to anything in international politics or domestic politics or any region of the world, and certainly nothing whatever to do with the Middle East or Egypt or Palestine or Iraq in 1917. And to purport that that's what that book is an outrageous falsehood.

Phillips doesn't claim to have read the book. He cites an article in the London Times that makes the charge that Bush is reading this crusade-inspiring work. Yes, Chambers calls the reader and the believer to a great struggle. That is true. And the great struggle is with the sin and sloth within oneself. It is completely a book of

```
personal devotions, urging personal spirituality
and leading to personal actions.
```

I find it quite moving to realize that a man whom I feared and distrusted was, in fact, moving along the same Christian path that I would follow a few years later. While it's quite possible to explain this convergence rationally—after all, Kurth and I have many common interests and experiences--it's also difficult to escape the sensation that God is always working in mysterious and subtle ways.

Soaring Debt, Uncertain Politics, and the Financialization of the United States

This chapter begins a three-part section on debt and financial policy, and I will say right at the outset that I expect that I will have far less to criticize about Phillips's analysis of these problems. My predisposition is to agree with him. I think the Bush budgetary policy of "spend without limit on defense and, by the way, cut taxes for the wealthy" is insane, and I would be a lot happier if we still had a budget surplus. It's certainly not at all clear that we have gotten value for money the more than 1 trillion dollars in extra debt we have incurred as a result of 9/11, the Iraq war, and the afterglow of the Internet bubble.

If you think of the expenditure as a form of social insurance, it has worked so far, in that we've spent a ton of money but we haven't had any more 9/11s. On the other hand, we've spent *far* more than it would have cost to repair the damage from 9/11 and do nothing further. On the question of value-for-money in the Bush budget, my judgment is that the jury's still out. Those who oppose the Iraq war would say that, on the financial counts alone, there are **twelve angry men glaring at George W. Bush as he awaits sentencing.**

ANOTHER AUTHOR WITH A VESTED INTEREST offers the epigraph for this chapter, with James Medoff and Andrew Harless opining that "Debt, directly or indirectly, has decayed the very soul of America." It's interesting that I read this passage on the very day that President George W. Bush said, in defending the war in Iraq,

> If we ever give up the desire to help people
> who live in freedom, we will have lost our soul as
> a nation, as far as I'm concerned.[37] (August 21,
> 2006)

Which **soul threat** do I find more serious? Well, if you have too much debt, you have no freedom. On the other hand, if you have no freedom, you may still have debt imposed upon you by the state.

Which soul threat do I find more plausible? Frankly, the debt threat seems a lot more real to me than the hypothetical danger to our nation of giving up on Iraq.   If the United States winds up walking away from Iraq, there will be a lot of negative practical and strategic consequences, but there's nothing to stop us from choosing to fight again for a different, more winnable, cause. As my dad loves to say, the motto of the Zimmermans is "**brave men run in our family.**"

PHILLIPS INTRODUCES THE *NYT*-COINED PHRASE "BORROWER-INDUSTRIAL COMPLEX" at the beginning of this chapter, and I love it.

IT'S WHAT PHILLIPS DOES *NOT* SAY IN THIS CHAPTER that I have a quarrel with. He spends a great deal of time talking about the "borrower industrial complex," debt, and the financial-insurance-real estate (FIRE) sector of the economy. To listen to Phillips, you'd think that they represent the entire U.S. economy.   While he spends a great deal of time complaining about the disconnection between "financialization" and the "real economy," you get the sense that Phillips wouldn't know the real economy **if it bit him in the ass.** Contrary to the impression Phillips gives, there is still a vibrant real economy in this country which has seen vast and remarkable transformations for the better in the past thirty years.

---

[37]http://www.cbsnews.com/stories/2006/08/22/ap/politics/
mainD8JLE7V80.shtml

What he dismisses in passing as the "tech bubble" did actually create huge gains in wealth for many families. The advent of the Internet essentially amounted to a "double or triple your income" card for everyone with any knack for abstract analytical thinking. While I would agree that this leaves many (most?) members of the traditional Democratic labor coalition behind, it is nevertheless a significant part of the "real" economy. And it would be wrong to dismiss all the "consumption" gains of the past thirty years as meaningless. Surely it is worth something that we all have our own PCs, DVDs, and MP3 players now...

Another problem with Phillips's approach in this chapter is that **he tends to focus on slices that favor his thesis.** For example, he makes a big deal that the financial services sector eclipsed manufacturing as a source of corporate profit and GDP, going from 10.9 vs. 29.3% in 1950 to 20.4% vs. 12.7 in 2003. **What about the remaining sectors of the economy**, which went from roughly 60% in 1950 to 70% in 2003? Surely one could argue that the trend across all sectors was diversification, which is generally regarded as a good thing.

"DEBT HAS LONG BEEN A TOOL OF ECONOMIC AND POLITICAL MANAGEMENT," Phillips writes, and I fully agree. High levels of debt function as a way of forcing people to toe the line, be good corporate citizens, and to avoid the social, political, and financial risk of being without a steady job. It would be interesting to conduct a study to see the lifetime effects of indebtedness on propensity for entrepreneurship. I'm guessing that people who are held back by debt are dramatically less likely to become entrepreneurs. What's interesting about this line of argument, though, is that it suggests that Republicans, by tightening the bankruptcy laws, are to some degree reducing the growth of their own core constituency, small business; and that they could steal a march on the Democrats by positioning themselves as the party that reduces the debt load for people in their twenties and thirties.

It's a bit annoying, though, that Phillips doesn't point out that employer-funded health insurance is also a means of social control that forces employees **to kowtow to The Man.** Once again, it would be nice for Phillips to acknowledge that there are many different means of social control and that debt, while a major problem , is not the only problem on the table.

Phillips touches on the interplay of religion and debt by suggesting that "George W. Bush, struggling with his succession of debt-ridden or nearly insolvent ... oil businesses ... turned to God[38]" and that many other Americans may have done the same thing as "nooses seemed to tighten" around them.

Speaking of religion, it is rather remarkable that at no point in this chapter does Phillips mention perhaps the most famous sentence in the English language that mentions the word debt:

```
       This, then, is how you should pray: 'Our Father
   in heaven,   hallowed be your name, your kingdom
   come, your will be done on earth as it is in
   heaven. Give us today our daily bread. Forgive us
   our debts, as we also have forgiven our debtors.
   And lead us not into temptation, but deliver us
   from the evil one.'
```

Contrary to what you might think from reading *American Theocracy,* Christians have had quite a few wise and sensible things to say about debt.

THE NEXT SECTION is *The Precarious Trajectory of American Debt* and I will say that this is indeed a very scary section, full of alarming factoids.

---

[38] I have deliberately omitted from this quotation Phillips's unChristian comment that Bush "found alcohol first."

- The national debt: $7.8 trillion

- Net foreign indebtedness: $3.3 trillion

- "Household deficit," the amount by which Americans' **outgo exceeded their income:** $1.04 for every $1.00

- Credit-market debt: 287 percent of GDP, higher than in 1929.

Ok, I'm terrified! How'd we get into this mess? Phillips blames it on two main groups of people: **Republicans and Alan Greenspan.** The Clinton era now appears like a halcyon era of financial prudence, although Phillips does points out that current accounts deficits (international debt) rose throughout the period. After the collapse of the Internet boom, Phillips argues, **"Chairman Bubbles"** stimulated the economy with low interest rates to keep the housing bubble from popping. Only thus was the Bush team able to afford its insane plan of massive war time spending combined with tax cuts. Phillips incisively observes that the Bush-Greenspan package represented "a gamble against human nature on ... the debt-management capacities of the Federal Reserve Board and the public-spiritedness of the financial-services industry."

As a devoted reader of *The Wall Street Journal,* a solid Republican, and a fully indebted member of borrower-industrial complex, I must agree that the financial-services industry has little or no public spirit. Phillips wisely points out that the FIRE industry provides a much thinner slice of jobs to the economy than the manufacturing industry did in its heyday: 8 million out of the national workforce of 131 million as opposed to 17 million out of 68 million in 1960. Yet although fewer average Joes are represented by the FIRE sector, its political power is if anything more immense than the good old days of "what was good for General Motors was good for the country." Phillips's eye for the telling one-liner works well for him here as he deftly deploys James Carville's great comment that "if he could be reincarnated, he'd want to come back as the bond market because it was so powerful."

The four leading lifetime patrons of George W. Bush, according to a 2004 study by the Center for Public Integrity that Phillips cites, were:

- Morgan Stanley

- Merrill Lynch

- Pricewaterhouse Coopers

- MBNA

I like Bush, voted for him twice and would probably do so again, but I have to agree that this list sheds some light on the abortive 2005 effort for Social Security privatization.

I LIKED THE "MACRO" HISTORICAL PERSPECTIVE that Phillips brings to the role of public finance as "a major source of great fortune through late medieval times." The reason I like this historical factoid more than the ones about Spain and the Netherlands is that it is based on a *comprehensive* study done by *The Wall Street Journal* for "a millennial retrospect on great wealth holders."

"GREED IS GOOD," Oliver Stone's Gordon Gekko famously declared, and although Wall Street "stars" like Gekko and Henry Blodgett no longer rule the Olympian skies of business journalism, I believe Phillips is absolutely right in declaring that the financial-services industry is still extremely important to the United States, resting "less on glamorous individuals and more **on a perverse interplay of magnitude and jeopardy.**" As a result, Phillips argues, the government has applied "large green liquidity Band-Aids" at every threat to the interest of the financial sector. **Phillips persuaded me** that this amounts to the government "picking winners", which is generally regarded as a no-no by free-market advocates, but he did not persuade me that this amounts to the government picking finance as the "ascendant sector" in the American economy. He seems to be forgetting that there are a number of other sectors that have also been enormous beneficiaries of government policy— health, defense, and transportation, to name only a few. I'm not sure that it makes any sense to talk about an "ascendant" sector. If you're saying that they're **first at the trough,** yes, I'm with you so far, but that's not to say that **a coalition of slightly less ginormous pigs** could not displace them on any given issue: in which case what does it mean to be "ascendant"? It just means you get your way most of the time, and slightly more often than the next guy in line. That's quite a bit less exciting than the one-dimensional portrait Phillips paints.

SOMETIMES PHILLIPS SLIPS TOO MUCH INTO PHILLIPS-SPEAK, as when he condemns American policy makers for "staking the American future on a sector with no record of sustaining earlier global economic hegemonies." Say what? Didn't you just get through reminding us that the finance sector has been an engine of vast wealth since medieval times? Didn't you see the little blurb at the end of the Merrill Lynch ad saying "past performance is no guarantee of future performance"? It seems perfectly reasonable to me to argue that finance might be the dominant economic sector in the next century, given the global unprecedented flows of capital, et cetera, et cetera. Who knows whether that will happen, but it's certainly not persuasive, on this type of issue, to say that just because it's never happened before, it will never happen now.

"DEBTOR SOCIETY, CREDIT-CARD NATION" is the title of the next section, and it sends chills down my spine, as far too much of my family's net worth is tiedp in credit-card debt. Still, things could be worse for me, as Phillips cheerfully reminds us:

- Nearly one-third of bankruptcy filers owed an entire year's salary on their credit cards;

- One "unlucky" American filed for bankruptcy every fifteen seconds in 2004;

- The household debt-service ratio in 2005 was 13.4 percent of after-tax income;

- Interest-only loans amounted for 60 percent of new mortgages in California;

- "those over sixty-five ... have 'the fastest-growing home debt, but also the fastest-growing share of bankruptcy filings ...'"

- "Between 1981 and 2001, medical-related bankruptcies increased by 2,200 percent." (Excuse my French, but aren't the health insurance companies just a bunch of **absolute bastards?**)

- By 2005, "nearly forty percent of the typical [credit-card] issuer's came from penalty fees." (Parlez-vous **Français?**)

The gist: bad things are already happening to individuals, and a lot more bad things will happen **if the credit industry falls off a cliff:**

```
"By 2005" [financial-sector debt was] three
times as much as the Nasdaq equity vaporized" [in
the Internet bubble].
```

Ok, Kevin, you scared me.

ADVANCING THE DEBATE:

1. Remember that the real American economy is hugely complex and diverse. No matter how stinky the finance sector is, it's only a (sizable) piece of the puzzle.

2. Remember the sectors that Phillips doesn't talk about—entertainment, energy, defense, health, medicine, services...

3. Remember that, despite the dire picture painted in this chapter, a great many Americans have actually been employed in productive labor for the last half-century, and vast new wealth has been created.

4. Pay down your own credit card debt: pronto!

Debt: History's Unearned Lesson

Smart-Alec Summary: Uh-oh!

I HAVE ALWAYS BELIEVED IN THE VALUE OF STUDYING HISTORY, so I was both tickled and annoyed to see that in this chapter, Kevin Phillips has pretty much reduced it to two sentences:

> Because the past repeats only in general
> resemblance, there is always something different,
> something new. This truth, together with the usual
> effects of the passage of time, makes it easy for
> later generations to dismiss any awkward
> precedents … (298)

The rhetorical device that Phillips is using here might be called **inoculation.** By acknowledging that there is always something different between then and now, and putting forward the idea that people tend to dismiss "awkward" precedents, he is protecting the predictive value of his beloved histories of Spain, the Netherlands, and Great Britain. Unfortunately, as I have said in earlier chapters, and will not repeat at great length here, **I just don't buy it.** There are too many huge differences between the world political economy at 1500 AD, 1700 AD, and 1900 AD and the world economy today for me to feel comfortable with any cyclical interpretation of the nature of hegemonic decline.

Nevertheless, I loved the examples of **globe-spanning self-aggrandizement** that Phillips was able to find in the rhetorical flourishes offered by Spanish, Dutch, and British jingoists. To be sure, American discussion of international affairs has been full of similarly smug and overheated verbiage since the beginning of the Republic, and particularly so since the end of the Second World War.

What exactly does that prove, though? It's always easy to find examples of fatuous thinking; in this case, smugness. The question is always whether the fatuity is **the signal or the noise.** I have to admit that in the previous chapter Phillips persuaded me that **the debt problem is signal,** not noise. I cannot say the same about his theory of the lifecycle of world economic hegemony, as explained in the next section: *"Finance: the Endgame of Champions,"* which might be summarized as **finance is for losers.** Phillips spends eight pages expounding on how the financial sector didn't do much to help the Spanish economy, five hundred years ago, but never really gets past this quote he offers from Alan Greenspan:

> "Is it important for an economy to have manufacturing? There is a big debate on that."

Well, yes, that is a pretty important question ... I only wish Phillips had answered it here (he tackles it in the section after next).

AS A WORD-LOVER AND FRANCOPHILE, I MUST APPLAUD THE NEXT SECTION, in which Phillips introduces the lovely word *"rentier,"* or person living off unearned income, which in modern-day parlance means something like **trust-fund baby** or **capitalist parasite.** The key thing about rentiers, in Phillips's view, is that they **follow the money:** they put their capital where they can get the highest return, regardless of whether it is in domestic industries in foreign, so their interests are no longer aligned with the communities within which they live. As a lifelong Michigander, this sounds like a very familiar story.

PHILLIPS SPENDS SOME TIME TRACING THE HISTORY OF DEBT TO GDP RATIOS of Spain and England, and winds up in a rather awkward position because his historical record shows that leading economic powers have frequently overcome high ratios of debt to GDP. To deal with these facts, he has to resort to questionable argument: "nations [can] marshal ... debt-defying high-wire ... comebacks during their youth ... but they [become] less resilient in later years." Argument from organismal analogy is tricky business; do nations really age like animals?

THE SAME QUESTIONABLE ORGANISMAL ANALOGY underlies the next section, in which Phillips argues that postindustrialism "may be more a quest for genteel retirement than a real economics-based future for a major power." He finds some great quotes from early 20th-Century British figures who were hoping that Great Britain would become "the financial and commercial service center to the world." These British experts do sound an awful lot like modern-day American lawyers with **a glorious vision of first London, now New York as the overpriced services capital of the world.**

But wait a minute! Is it not true that London is still one of the top ten, or perhaps top five, or top two, financial centers in the world? (And a pretty darned nice place to live, too). So was the British strateg entirely mistaken?

Evidently, Phillips would prefer that the United States should model itself on powers like **Germany, Switzerland, and Japan** which have high savings rates, high current-accounts surpluses, and strong manufacturing economies. He seems oblivious that a) these countries are far more homogeneous than the United States and b) they all have their fair share of major structural defects. (And isn't Switzerland the quintessence of a country that relies on financial services?)

Phillips does make an excellent point when he observes that **the industrial era is not over.** In fact, if you think about those **3.2 billion capitalists in India and China as buyers of industrial goods,** the industrial era may be just beginning. Do we really want to be on the postindustrial sidelines while all that money is being made?

Phillips is less credible when he decries American military deindustrialization. He's correct in bringing up examples of key technologies where the United States may no longer be able to meet its own manufacturing needs, but **c'mon:** after the preceding three hundred pages of worrying about military adventurism, does Phillips really expect us to believe he's genuinely worried about defense tech?

ADAM SMITH WAS WRONG and "the invisible hand" is more like "**an invisible foot** kicking society in the shins." (The source of that last phrase? Warren Buffett.) **We need more industrial policy,** Phillips thinks, on the Asian model. Oh, good! That's *just* what we need. Am I the only one who sees "industrial policy" as basically a power battle between lobbyists?

What have we learned from this rather short chapter? According to Phillips,

1. History is **cyclical,** except when it isn't.

2. Finance is for **losers.**

3. The **Spanish Empire** sucked.

4. **Rentiers** suck.

5. **Debt** sucks.

6. **Adam Smith** sucks.

7. **Industrial policy**, surprisingly, doesn't suck.

ADVANCING THE DEBATE

How do we talk intelligently about the role of industrial policy in the American economy? It seems to me that it would be handy to have a little bar chart that shows the dollars spent on lobbying Congress per sector . So here it is, via OpenSecrets.org.

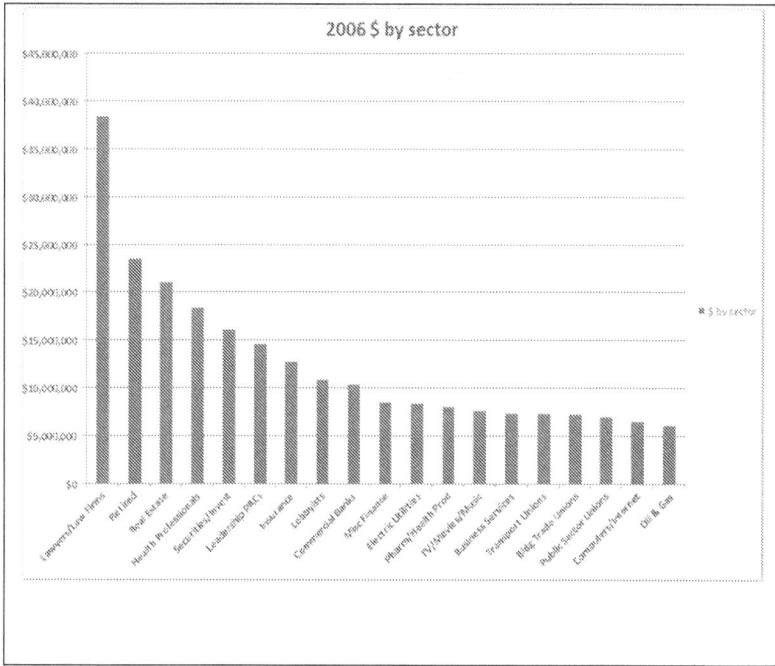

2006 $ by sector

Just as Phillips projects, real estate, securities, insurance, lobbyists, banks, and finance are at the top of the list. Looking at this, I have to agree that Phillips is right: **the FIRE sector is a danger to the commonwealth.** But remember: industrial policy means taking resources and preference away from one sector, and giving them to another.

1. Be careful what you wish for ...

2. Let's remember that for everything Adam Smith's invisible hand fails to explain, there are a dozen things that it explains very well.

3. Let's not talk about the Spanish empire!

Serial Bubbles and Foreign Debt Holders: American Embarrassment and Asian Opportunity

SMART-ALEC SUMMARY: All your debts are belong to us.[39]

THE FIRST EPIGRAPH QUOTES THE SCARY STATISTIC that the net savings rate for the U.S. has fallen to only 1.2 percent, from a peak of 8.5 percent in 1981. If we are to take this literally, Americans, on average, are 8x less financially secure than they were in 1981. Can that be exactly right?

THE SECOND EPIGRAPH MAKES US SOUND LIKE REAL DUMBASSES compared to the British, who were a creditor empire in 1914, whereas we are a debtor empire. The obvious retort is the playground one: if they're so smart, why aren't they still in charge?

BACK IN THE DEPARTMENT OF SPURIOUS LOGIC, Phillips attempts to terrify us with the thought that "persistent newspaper headlines about debt are innately worrisome." Let's run this through the reality processor. Are "persistent newspaper headlines about" bad things "innately worrisome"? Well, no, they aren't, unless your main source of information is newspapers...

TO BE FAIR, though, this chapter looks **downright prescient** in light of the 2007 mortgage credit crisis, as Phillips begins with a

---

[39] For a history of the "all your bases are belong to us" Internet meme, see http://en.wikipedia.org/wiki/All_your_base_are_belong_to_us.

warning about the debt-loaded U.S. consumer as "the wheelhorse of the world economy."

Phillips correctly anticipates that "currency weakness is rarely a good sign," and worries about the consequences of Asian countries holding so much of our debt. It's interesting, though, that he doesn't seem to have anticipated that the consequence of all this overextended foreign debt has not been to start a "run on America", but instead to stimulate calls from European governments that they should have more of a say in regulating U.S. financial instruments. It's striking to me that the Europeans have stopped well short of saying "let us regulate the world economy": they're just saying "you keep on regulating it, but we want you to be more accountable and transparent." In other words, the central role of the U.S. turns out to be less readily transferable than Phillips would have us believe.

HE IS RIGHT ABOUT THE SCALE OF OUR VULNERABILITY, though: he suggests that most of the almost $40 trillion in credit market debt is vulnerable, and the mortgage crisis seems to bear him out. He also notes that the U.S. must consider private debts as almost on a par with public debts, because the history of major financial disasters in the U.S. is a history of government bailouts and interventions.

MY SYMPATHIES ARE COMPLETELY WITH PHILLIPS in the next major section, which he calls *The Indentured American Household*. Suffice it to say that considering the state of my family's finances, it would be intellectually dishonest for me to do anything but nod soberly in agreement. We are up to our eyeballs in debt to a handful of major financial corporations, and indentured is not too strong a word for it.

Does it make you angry that **fees represented 39 percent of credit-card issuer profits in 2004?** It makes me furious, and I appreciate Phillips for telling me about it.

Does it scare you that the amount people charged increased by 350 percent from 1900 to 2003? It scares me, and it should. During this time, while my income increased by a factor of six, my debt went from 0 to huge. To be sure, a lot of that was my own fault. But some of it is due to a favorable public policy climate. Where were Bill Clinton and the Democratic party during this time period? Asleep at the wheel, evidently, practicing "the politics of personal ~~distraction~~ destruction," nibbling out "achievable" victories. **Bastards,** all of them...

"THE INVISIBLE FOOT" IS THE NOT-TERRIBLY-EUPHONIOUS phrase coined by Warren Buffett as a play on Adam Smith's "invisible hand" to describe the negative effect of "casino-type markets" and "hair-trigger investment management" on a forward-moving economy. Phillips uses the "Invisible Foot" as the title of the next section, and (like many other smart people before him) cites Buffett as an authority for skepticism about complex financial instruments. It's easy to invoke one of the world's richest men as an authority on a financial issue, but I think this convenient Buffettmania needs a bit more scrutiny. Buffett owns a portfolio of very boring, financially sound companies that are **intrinsically conservative.** Does Phillips really want a public policy that makes Coca-Cola and Microsoft happy? Does anyone?

PHILLIPS IS VERY NEGATIVE ABOUT SECURITIZED INSTRUMENTS, which struck me as a Luddite position, at least until the mortgage-credit crisis. I think it's interesting that the gap in perspectives here is as much a psychographic one as a political or financial one. People who are **analytically gifted** love these clever ideas to repackage things and virtualize them. Folks from the "old school" (like Samuel Johnson" like things to be concrete.[40]

---

[40] "The philosopher and churchman George Berkeley, if I understand him correctly, put forward the contention that nothing is real, in the sense that the universe exists only in our perceptions. It was commented at the time that this

MORE SCARY FACTS: in 2005 the household debt-service ratio (debt payments to disposable income) reached an all-time high of 13.4 percent. **What's yours?** Ours is higher, but we just purchased a new home, so most of our mortgage payments are interest.

WILLIE NELSON SANG "YOU WERE ALWAYS ON MY MIND", and Kevin Phillips might as well be singing it to Asia. In the next section, *And Now, Over to Asia,* he tells us:

- "Almost all" of the $399 billion in U.S. assets purchased by foreign governments in 2004 came from Asia.

- "Since 2000, all of the net new supply of Treasuries has been purchased by nonresidents, and about 80 to 90% by foreign central banks."

- Asian central banks are motivated by a desire for "dominance" over lucrative export markets.

Again, the obvious question: if Asian central banks are so smart, why aren't they running the world? The obvious answer is that Korea is too small, Japan is too insular, China is too autocratic, and none of them are trusted enough by the smart money around the world.

WILL WAR MAKE US GO PFFFFT? Phillips thinks so, as he argues in the section on *War: The Military and Economic Unmasking of Global Hegemons.*

> "The annals of the leading world economic
> powers … show a clear pattern of major wars

---

theory, while underlined radical, could not be refuted, any more than it could be proved. Samuel Johnson, however, took a different view. When asked by Boswell what he thought of Berkeley's theory that matter may not, in fact, exist, Johnson kicked hard at a stone and stated, "I refute him thus!" http://www.everything2.com/index.pl?node_id=670519

> playing a central role in the upending of one
> hegemon and the emerging of another." (339)

Reasonable enough. Could Iraq be such a war?

Kevin Phillips's examination of the historical record suggests that the international realignments that crippled previous empires came from global wars. Iraq is a horrible mess that has done nothing for the U.S. standing around the globe, and "victory" seems further away than ever. My dad's former student Lieutenant General William Odom, former director of the famously secretive National Security Agency, told Congress that Iraq was "the biggest strategic mistake in U.S. history."

But Iraq is not a global war, and the conflict is taking place *there*, not here. And-here's a contrarian thought sure to appall most of my readers-there's an argument to be made that the Rumsfeld/Bush strategy on limiting the number of troops in country was *right*.

In my view, the troop limit was fundamentally a political decision to manage risk, based on a rational calculation that actual victory in Iraq was not worth the potential risks of going "all in" to Iraq. In other words, no single hand in the Great Game is worth all your chips. **What if we had deployed 500,000 troops to Iraq in 2003 and the country still wasn't pacified?** What if, instead of setting off a nuke to get attention in 2006, North Korea had decided to invade South Korea? (When you get right down to it, he Democratic People's Republic of Korea is **all about acting out...**)

LAW PROFESSORS LOVE TO TELL THEIR STUDENTS: "DON'T FIGHT THE FACTS." This is an important adage because students often respond to challenging legal issues by subtly modifying the facts of the case to make it easier to reach a desired result. **Fighting the facts** will certainly seem familiar to many critics of the Bush administration, but liberals are not immune to it, either. Iraq isn't a global war, and

Phillips's argument doesn't support seeing it as the end of U.S. hegemony.

THE LAST HUGE THREAT THAT PHILLIPS DISCUSSES in this chapter is the risk of the eventual bankruptcy of Social Security and Medicare. Surprisingly, he's relatively cheerful about those situations, basically because he thinks the time horizons are too long to worry about. Phillips says he is worried about three major threats: financial irresponsibility (in terms of debt), oil dependency, and radical religion.

An interesting list. What about **terrorism?** Global **warming?** Nuclear **Armageddon?** Pandemic? **The Four Horsemen of the Apocalypse?** And don't forget **the Republican Party**, the subject of the final chapter of this book.

ADVANCING THE DEBATE

1. I have to say that that by devoting most of this chapter to the debt problem Phillips did a true public service that advanced the debate very significantly. We need to keep the heat on this issue!

2. I think we need to spend less time worrying about Asian debtholders per se and more time worrying about encouraging the growth of transparent, accountable, democratic, like-minded governments in Asia. The worst thing we have to worry about from Europe is Eurocrats regulating us to death. **We should be so lucky** with Asia.

3. A fundamental flaw with Phillips's approach in this book is that he is singling out three (arguably) related dangers, connecting them, inflating them, and ignoring all the others. In my view, **a much more systematic approach is required,** beginning with defining what exactly it is that we want to enhance and protect (what *is* good about America? Is it our role as global hegemon? I think not), then

examining all the necessities and risks related to our actual goals, not our factitious goals.

The Erring Republican Majority

SMART-ALEC SUMMARY: It's the Republicans, stupid.

I only wish our problems were this simple.

EPIGRAPH #1: Paul Volcker saying something scary about "disturbing trends." Ok, first question: **who's Paul Volcker?** I remember, of course, but doesn't he seem like someone who was **last relevant about twenty billion years ago?** When you boil the quote down to its actual information content, there's nothing to it except anecdotal fear, uncertainty, and doubt.

EPIGRAPH #2: An economist at Morgan Stanley says we've outsourced our financing to Asia. As I commented in the last chapter, if Asian finance ministers are so smart, why aren't they running Europe?

EPIGRAPH #3: Matthew Simmons, author of *Twilight In the Desert*, complaining that there is not a single contingency plan to address how the world will continue to function smoothly once it is clear that Saudi Arabian oil production has peaked. Excuse me: there is a really darned good contingency plan that has been operating on a global basis for the last two hundred years. It's **called the free market,** and markets have been making the possibility of oil shortages since 1973. **Remember basic capitalism 101? Markets are efficient.** They're not perfect, but they're certainly a lot more efficient than book authors and think-tanks...

EPIGRAPH #4: Garry Wills worrying about faith-based federal agencies. The whole faith-based thing seems like a somewhat remote worry with the advent of a Democratic Congress in 2006 and the distinct possibility of a Democratic President in 2009. Can it be that this whole thing about the "erring Republican majority"

was **a self-correcting problem?** That would be good news—
wouldn't it?

REPUBLICAN ARE BAD, AND BAD THINGS ARE THEIR FAULT, is the
message of the introduction to this chapter. "Suffice it to say that
the nation's most troublesome circumstances to the fealty of an
erring Republican majority to its most important constituencies." In
other words, not only are Republicans bad, but they are stupid.

The first section of the chapter is called *After Iraq: Oil, Debt, and
the Dollar.* (I can hardly blame Phillips for failing to anticipate that
by 2008 there would still be no "after Iraq.") Phillips's main
point is that "after Iraq" there was no increase in oil production, so
that oil prices increased, OPEC nations reduced their dollar
holdings, American debt rose, and things became even more **scary.**
"In both oil consumption and currency management, the clock of
American vulnerability was ticking."

If America is so vulnerable, why didn't the mortgage crisis cause
everyone to flee the dollar?

APPARENTLY, RELIGIOUS PEOPLE ARE BOTH BAD AND STUPID. In the
first paragraph of the next section, *Religion and the Republican
Coalition,* Phillips quotes an invisible factoid that 30 to 40 percent
of the Republican coalition believes in the Rapture. In the second
paragraph, he reports that 42 percent of Americans described
themselves to survey takers as born-again. He doesn't appear to see
the inconsistency between these two facts. To put it simply, any
pastor would tell you that more people believe in being "born
again" than believe in the rapture. "Born again" is a very broad
umbrella category that's easy to claim. The number of people who
identify themselves as born again is much, more larger than the
number of people who make The Rapture the focus of their
worship, and larger still than the number who actually make daily
decisions on the assumption that the rapture is imminent.

In the remainder of the section, Phillips ponders the implications of religious politics for the Republican Presidential Primaries. At this writing, it's too early to tell whether Phillips is right that "theological correctness stands to be an Republican Achilles's heel... that forces the Republican party to lean too far to the right." On the one hand, religious conservatives are not exactly thrilled with the field so far. Sam Brownback is long gone, Rudy Giuliani is (at the moment) standing tall, and Mitt Romney supposedly believes that Joseph Smith was visited by an angel in upstate New York in 1820. (I have my doubts whether the Mitt Romney who was CEO of Bain & Company actually believes that.) the On the other hand, Fred Thompson is coming up strong. But genuinely religious people realize that Fred Thompson is no Billy Graham.

Phillips did not anticipate the primary schedule changes for 2008, which will probably make **TV, rather than religion, the dominant factor in determining the Republican candidate.** If you follow the "TV rules" theory, religion is probably going to be decisive in the Republican race only if one of the candidates makes a religiously themed gaffe. Otherwise, it will boil down to **name recognition, telegenicity, and dollars.**

Is THE DOLLAR A DEER? Apparently that's what have Phillips would believe, as he titles the next section *The Greenback at Bay.* This is really quite a telling metaphor, as the only things that are ever "at bay" in real life are hunted animals like deer. How much sense does it make compare an abstract, fungible medium of exchange to an animal? According to Phillips, Washington policy makers are ill-prepared for the "post-2001 surveillance of a hard-eyed Asian power elite: the central banks of creditor nations." There's really only one nation that matters here, and that's China, and as the consumer products crises of 2007 revealed, China's autocratic leaders are simply not administratively prepared to monitor their own economy, let alone anyone else's. The reality of the last twenty years is that the only significant challenge to U.S. financial and economic policy has come from the European Union. It is the

European Union that has succeeded in bringing the likes of Microsoft to heel (to use a animal metaphor myself) and it is the European Union that called for closer supervision of the U.S. financial sector after the mortgage crisis.

Phillips gives full rein to his Asia paranoia as he imagines the "blunt economic language in the conference rooms of Asian financiers":

> "Why don't the Americans take care of their industry and invest in it? Why do they dither over primitive and antiscientific religion? Why are their children so far behind our students?..."
> (361)

Do Asian financiers really talk like **James Bond villains?** Somehow I think that behind closed doors they are a lot more concerned with their own issues than they are with ours.

Phillips also seems willfully blind to the strengths of the American economy: its scale, its dynamism, its flexibility. A lot of those imaginary conversations in Asian cloakrooms are still about how to get a child into Harvard.

Where does the "erring Republican majority" come in? Phillips thinks an active governmental industrial policy is the answer to our problems, and it frustrates him that Republicans don't believe in it. The bottom line? **No one is listening to him.** According to Phillips, it's because "much of what the Republican party" stands for has become "based on faith, not reason."

THEY'RE NOT BEING RATIONAL! That might as well be the title of the next section, *Cultural and Political Fundamentalism: The Theology of U.S. Domestic and Foreign Policy.* Phillips strings together a series of poll findings to paint an alarming picture According to polls Phillips cites, 71 percent of evangelicals expect Armageddon, 63 percent call the state of Israel a fulfillment of the biblical prophecy of the second coming of Jesus, and 55% of white evangelical protestants consider "following religious principles" a top priority for foreign policy. Phillips jumps from there to the conclusion that "religion has been the principal denominator of the aggressiveness of the GOP rank and file in the Middle East."

In fact, a principal reason for middle American hostility to the Arab world is the Arab world's hostility to *us*. As Osama Bin Ladin is fond of reminding the world "**it's the policy, stupid.**" In this case, it's the Palestinian and Arab policy of suicide bombing that we find objectionable. Many Americans see the Middle East as the source of a great deal of violence, including, by the way, a particularly heinous act of aggression on 9/11. I gladly concede that it is rational to consider the violence as a natural consequence of a history of colonialism and oppression, but remember, in this section we are talking about what *conservative Americans* think. And what they think is that the violence between the Arab world and West is the Arab world's fault.

WE MIGHT WISH that conservative Americans would ask themselves more often "is this my fault in any way?" and we might observe that the idea that "it's the other guy's fault" is somewhat inconsistent with the Christian principles of the Sermon on the Mount—but that's my point. There is a big difference between what people say and what they actually believe. High-level answers to poll questions don't prove much unless you probe a lot deeper into tradeoffs and options.

Phillips casts a similarly skeptical eye on a variety of other religiously inspired policy stands the Bush administration has taken:

- Opposition to international organizations funding pro-abortion policies;

- Resistance to climate change policy

- Opposition to human stem-cell research

- Resistance to AIDS-mitigation strategies such as condoms and generic antiretroviral drugs

```
"What at first seems to be an unrelated
patchwork of incidents adds up to a theological
quilt." (368)
```

The common thread, Phillips believes, is the desire to turn back the clock and return women to a more subservient position. This, he believes, is bad, because it upsets Europeans.

PHILLIPS WORRIES TOO MUCH ABOUT WHAT OTHERS THINK. He correctly points out that many of the Bush Administration's socially conservative policies are not appealing to sophisticated international audiences. "Realistically these events and circumstances hardly encourage foreign bankers, diplomats or political leaders to buy and hold U.S. Treasury bonds" and otherwise believe in America. (370) But he doesn't answer the more fundamental question: **so what?**

IS IT THE GOAL OF OUR SOCIAL POLICY to satisfy the World Bank? **No.** Even after the embarrassing Wolfowitz episode, we still run the World Bank.

IS IT THE GOAL OF OUR SOCIAL POLICY to seek to harmonize our values with current European standards? **No..** Remember, this country was founded by people who fled from current European standards.

IS IT THE GOAL OF OUR SOCIAL POLICY to make foreign *leaders* happy? **No.** It's odd that the very people who are most opposed to molly-coddling conservative foreign leaders are most in favor of molly-coddling liberal foreign leaders..

Phillips wraps up this section by worrying that the "surprising religification" of the Republican party has become more of a danger than the secular excesses of the left. This danger seems less pressing in 2007, with the Democratic party in control of Congress and great optimism on the Democratic side of the Presidential race.

PHILLIPS RIGHTLY SOUNDS THE KLAXON warning of a future financial crisis in the next section, *Financialization: A Volckerian Götterdämmerung.* Or should I say *Völckerian*?

Flash-forward to 2007. Financialized mortgage instruments have produced a crisis. But wait a minute: the world hasn't ended. That's because **financial crises are routine.** There were financial crises in 1973 (remember OPEC?), 1987, 1998, 2001, and 2007. That's one every seven years. They happen, and the world doesn't end.

A VÖLCKERIAN OPERA is one in which the fat lady of misfortune does sing for the people of the United States.. Phillips thinks the fat lady will sing in the 2010s or 2020s, when all the things he has been worrying about for the previous three hundred and eighty-one pages finally happen. He also thinks that China's GDP may be as large as America's by 2025, and that a "serious contest" could ensue by the 2010s.

Phillips acknowledges that the downfall of American power and the ascendency of China could be "tragic," but, .looking on the bright side, "there is a fascination" with the implications of a new economic supremacy in Asia. Well, that's great, Kev... why don't you move on out to Shanghai? The reasons are obvious: **China is a homogenous, overcrowded, polluted, unregulated autocracy.** The "fascinating" advent of Chinese hegemony would be a disaster for the world. And there's more good news for opera lovers ... Kevin Phillips thinks things are going to get worse for America! In the final section of this chapter, *Secularism, Sclerotic Politics, and Disillusionment,* he explains why.

WHEN WE LOSE OUR EMPIRE, WE'RE GOING TO LOSE OUR FAITH. According to Phillips, the disillusionment of declining hegemony is what caused Spain, the Netherlands, and Great Britain to lose their religious faith. "It is not hard to imagine something similar happening in the United States by 2030 or 2040 as two or three decades of cynicism claim religious as well as economic and political victims."

This is a bizarre reading of history. Most people would attribute the decline of religious faith in former European hegemons to a whole host of factors that simply are not present in the United States. For example:

Europe, but not the United States, had a huge exodus of fervent religious believers beginning three-hundred plus years ago. The religious believers were going from Europe to the United States. (Similar to the firemen who were going up the staircases in the World Trade Center when everyone else was going down!)

Europe, but not the United States, has a long history of established state religions that have problematic ties with state authority.

Europe, but not the United States, has a long history of self-inflicted suicidal wars that don't resolve anything.

Phillips says at 383 that Europeans are beginning to think the United States is "undependable and even an altogether different culture from itself", as if difference and undependability were identical. Of course we are different, and that's a good thing. The decline of U.S. hegemony (which I agree is inevitable in *the long run*) will, as a result, play out differently in the U.S. than it did in Spain, the Netherlands, and Great Britain.

It bothers Phillips that **they don't like us.**

It bothers Phillips that **they think we're stupid.**

He thinks **it's our fault.**

> "Within the United States[the evangelical
> community] … have their own communication system

and culture built around belief, both religious
and scriptural..."

And he thinks **we're doomed.**

""The lesson of the past is that timely reforms
do not emerge, and deep, unanswerable national
issues generate weak and compromising politicians
or zealous bumblers."

I can't argue with him about that—which means that the real question is whether he is correct in his fundamental diagnosis of the United States as foolish and sclerotic. It's all a question of perspective: does the bad outweigh the good? Phillips's book is all about the bad, so you have to step outside its framework to remember that there is still great strength in the American system.

ADVANCING THE DEBATE

1.   **Don't focus on the "erring Republican majority"** as the source of all problems. For one thing, the GOP is no longer a Congressional majority. The current Democratic Congress, acting against a Republican President, has appeared remarkably ineffectual.

2.   **Don't assume that a Democratic President in 2009 will fix everything** (or for that matter, anything).. I have been reading Carl Bernstein's Hillary Clinton book, *A Woman In Charge,* and it is a sobering reminder that the last time the Democrats had both the Congress and the Presidency, in 1993-1994, they **imploded.**

3.   Don't assume that **all religious people are stupid.**

4.   Don't assume that **being popular with European elites is the sine qua non of a sensible foreign policy.**

5.   Remember that **there's good news as well as bad.**

Afterword: The Changing Presidential Coalition

SMART-ALEC SUMMARY: It's all about counting the votes.

Key quote:

> "Bluntly putting it, I believe that a careful electoral analysis shows that what can be called the Bush coalition is too narrow to govern successfully and was empowered to win only by a succession of odd circumstances in both 2000 and 2004."

Phillips, whose first book was *The Emerging Republican Majority* in 1969, is back on solid ground when it comes to counting votes. He breaks down the Republican Presidential coalition along religious lines. Republicans, according to Phillips, are strongest in four regional grouping:

- The Southern Baptist Convention

- Mormons

- Upper Midwest Protestanism, especially Lutherans

- Pentecostals.

Conversely, Republicans are weakest in states with:

- Relatively large Catholic populations

- Sizable Jewish constituencies

- High percentages of nonbelievers

- Smaller Protestant populations with high mainline ratios.

What this all translates to is that Republicans have **become the party of Jim Crow:**

> "the Republican coalition is starting to look
> like the reverse of the one that existed for
> generations after the Civil War..." (393)

If you were in any doubt about the racial implications, Phillips adds: "the pattern involves greater Republican strength ... in **'cracker'** northern Florida."

If Phillips is right, the Republicans have become **the party that lost the Civil War**. As he suggests, that's "an innately narrowed constituency", not likely to win elections consistently.

REPUBLICANS ARE SELF-DEFEATING FOOLS, Phillips suggests, as he argues that the GOP coalition is "fatally flawed from a national-interest standpoint." **Just too many dumb people in the base:**

> "Never before has a U.S. political coalition
> been so dominated by an array of outsider
> religious denominations caught up in biblical
> morality, distrust of science, and a global
> imperative of political and religious
> evangelism." (393)

As Phillips points out, not only is this bad for the country, it's bad for the oil and gas industries. "... much of the real world as seen by cosmopolitan energy geologists and executives cannot be publicly described in Republican politics." Awww...

Eventually, Phillips believes, God will turn on the Republicans, both in and out of Washington, "religious excess and overambition will become part of an epitaph for the twenty-first century United States", and the current GOP national coalition will "share in the ignominy." As a believing Christian, I have to say that this is outrageous: **the world's going to hell in a handbasket,** and it's all *our* fault?

ADVANCING THE DEBATE

1. Phillips is right that democracy is **all about counting** the votes.

2. Don't blame religious people for everything you dislike. It's hard enough to assemble a winning coalition, so don't exclude the majority of the population (at least, according to Phillips) by disrespecting them right out of the box.

3. In the United States, a winning coalition includes respect for the views and attitudes of evangelical Christians. The last person to be elected President without strong evangelical support was George W. Bush, 41, who ran against Michael Dukakis (possibly the least evangelically sympathetic candidate ever.)

4. Don't whine. **Think about how to assemble your own winning coalition**.

Why Publish With Nimble Books

Nimble Books LLC is an innovative publisher of timely material on topics ranging from Iraq and politics to Harry Potter and Dan Brown. We use electronic publishing technology to reach markets that are moving too fast for the large publishing conglomerates to address. Because our marketing strategy is tightly focused on the Internet, we look for titles that respond well to keyword searching in on-line markets, or on-line promotion via blogging.

We publish twelve titles per year and we are selective. We are looking for books that are substantially ahead of the curve in that they address emerging trends that are readily connected with large, literate on-line communities.

If you like what you see here and you have something similar on the shelf, or in the works, please visit the Nimble Books website and take a look at "Why Publish With Us" (http://www.nimblebooks.com/wordpress/why-publish-with-nimble-books/). Then send a proposal and sample chapters to wfz@nimblebooks.com.

Colophon

This book was produced using Microsoft Word and Adobe Acrobat. The cover was produced using The Gimp 2.0.2 with Ghostscript. The cover font is Palatino Linotype. The spine is Verdana.

Heading fonts and the body text inside the book are in Constantia, chosen because it is a nimble-looking font that is new enough to be fresh on the eyes. Quotations are in Consolas, a fixed width font chosen for similar reasons.

The American Heritage® Dictionary of the English Language, Fourth Edition, copyright © 2000 by Houghton Mifflin Company defines col·o·phon as follows:

```
An ancient Greek city of Asia Minor northwest
of Ephesus. It was famous for its cavalry.
```

Along the same lines, Webster's Revised Unabridged, copyright 1996, 1998, MICRA, Inc.:

```
\Col"o*phon\ (k[o^]l"[-o]*f[o^]n), n. [L.
colophon finishing stroke, Gr. kolofw`n; cf. L.
culmen top, collis hill. Cf. Holm.] An
inscription, monogram, or cipher, containing the
place and date of publication, printer's name,
etc., formerly placed on the last page of a book.
```

For a book of this nature, what better finishing stroke could there be than the last words of Jesus?

```
{It is done …}
```

E-Guide to Cleanrooms

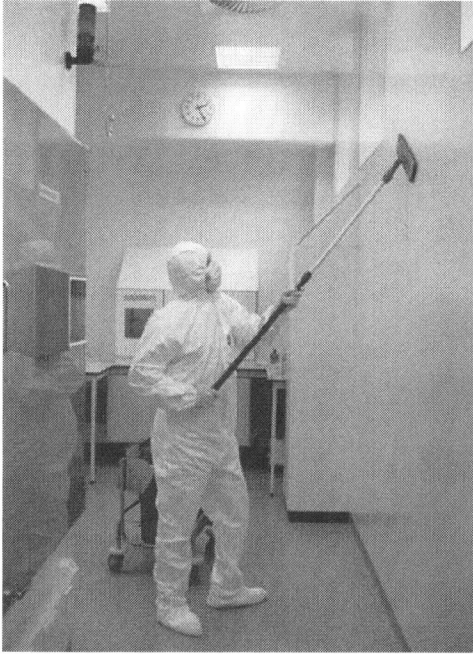

Dr. Tim Sandle

Published by Microbiology Solutions, St Albans, UK

Further information is available from:

www.pharmamicro.com

Dr. Tim Sandle

Tim Sandle is the Head of Microbiology at the UK Bio Products Laboratory. His role involves overseeing a range of microbiological tests, batch review, microbiological investigation and policy development. In addition, Tim is an honorary consultant with the School of Pharmacy and Pharmaceutical Sciences, University of Manchester and is a tutor for the university's pharmaceutical microbiology MS course. Tim is a chartered biologist and holds a first class honors degree in Applied Biology; a Masters degree in education; and a PhD in the safety testing of blood products.

Tim serves on several national and international committees relating to pharmaceutical microbiology and cleanroom contamination control (including the ISO cleanroom standards), and he has acted as a spokesperson for several microbiological societies. He is a committee member of the UK and Irish microbiology society Pharmig and editor of its newsletter. Tim has written over one hundred book chapters, peer reviewed papers and technical articles relating to microbiology. In addition, Tim runs an on-line microbiology blog (www.pharmig.blogspot.com).

Other books by Tim Sandle available on Amazon

Current Perspectives on Environmental Monitoring (2010)

Microbiology and Sterility Assurance in Pharmaceuticals and Medical Devices (2011) (with Madhu Raju Saghee and Edward Tidswell)

The CDC Handbook: A Guide to Cleaning and Disinfecting Cleanrooms (2012)

Pharmaceutical Microbiology Glossary (2012)

E-Guide to Cleanrooms

Introduction

This pocket guide has been developed in order to provide a short and informative guide to cleanrooms. Cleanrooms provide critical environments for both sterile and non-sterile pharmaceutical manufacturing.

The guide is divided into different sections. The first section looks at cleanrooms; different grades of cleanrooms and the important aspects of physical control. The second part looks at cleanroom classification. The third part discusses contamination control and environmental monitoring. The fourth part lists the important cleanroom parameters required by the regulatory standards.

Cleanrooms are highly controlled environments where the air quality is monitored to ensure the extreme standards of cleanliness required for the manufacture of pharmaceutical, electronic and healthcare goods. These stringent standards usually require high fresh air rates, extensive filtering, temperature and humidity control - all of which results in increased energy usage. Protection from uncontrolled ingress of external ambient air is achieved by creating a pressure differential between the cleanroom and its surroundings.

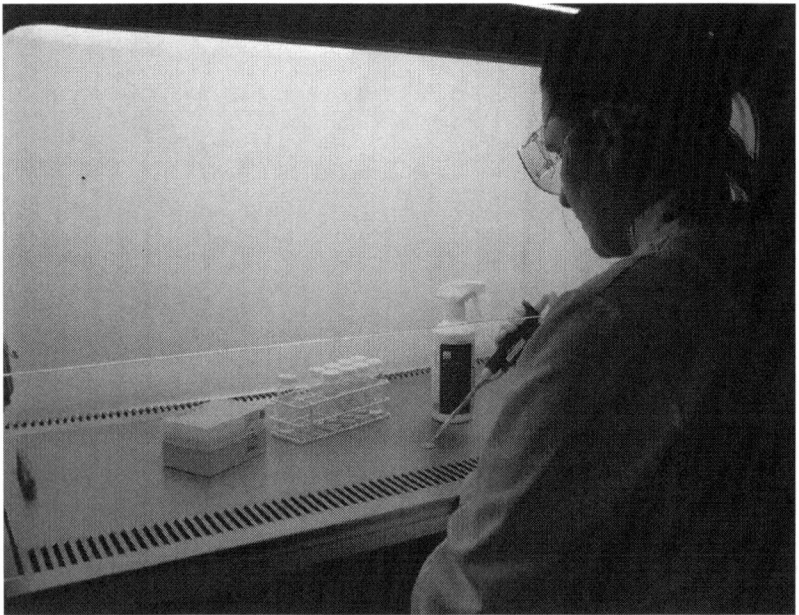

Photograph: Technician working in a clean air device

Contamination control is the primary consideration in cleanroom design; however the relationships between contamination control and airflow are not well understood. Contaminants such as particles or microbes are primarily introduced to cleanrooms by people although processes in cleanrooms may also introduce contamination. During periods of inactivity or when people are not present, it is possible to reduce airflow and maintain cleanliness conditions. To design the cleanroom, the following factors must be accounted for:

- Minimize clean space
- Correct cleanliness level
- Optimal air change rate
- Consider use of mini-environments
- Optimize ceiling coverage
- Consider cleanroom protocol and cleanliness class
- Minimize pressure drop (air flow resistance)
- Location of large air handlers – close to end use
- Adequate sizing and minimize length of ductwork
- Provide adequate space for low pressure drop air flow
- Low face velocity
- Use of variable speed fans
- Optimizing pressurization
- Consider air flow reduction when unoccupied
- Efficient components
- Face velocity
- Fan design
- Motor efficiency
- HEPA filters differential pressures (ΔP)
- Fan-filter efficiency
- Electrical systems that power air systems

The performance of a cleanroom is defined by a set of complex interactions between the airflow, sources of contamination and heat, position of vents, exhausts and any objects occupying the space. Consequently changes to any of these elements will potentially affect the operation of the cleanroom and could invalidate aspects of the room design.

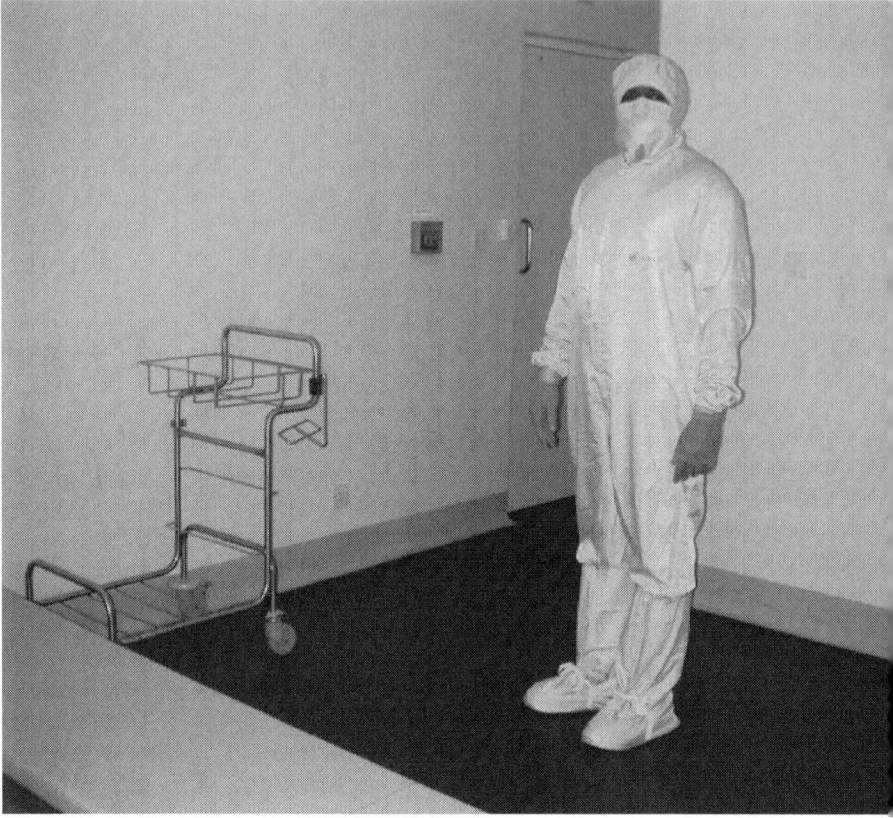

Photograph: Operator in a changing room

Part A: Introduction to cleanrooms

What are cleanrooms?

Clean rooms and zones are typically classified according to their use (the main activity within each room or zone) and confirmed by the cleanliness of the air by the measurement of particles. Cleanrooms are used in several industries including the manufacture of pharmaceuticals and in the electronics industry. For pharmaceutical cleanrooms, air cleanliness is either based on EU GMP guidance for aseptically filled products and the EU GMP alphabetic notations are adopted; or by using the International Standard ISO14644, where numerical classes are adopted. The cleanliness of the air is controlled by an HVAC system (Heating, Ventilation and Air-Conditioning).

The key aspect is that the level of cleanliness is controlled.

A more specialised meaning is:

"A room with control of particulates and set environmental parameters. Construction and use of the room is in a manner to minimise the generation and retention of particles. The classification is set by the cleanliness of the air" (as defined in ISO 14644-1).

By prescribing a grade or a class to a clean room, the areas are then regarded as controlled environments. A controlled environment is:

"Any area in an aseptic process system for which airborne particulate and microorganism levels are controlled to specific levels to the activities conducted within that environment" (Institute of Validation Technology Dictionary).

For EU GMP the typical room uses and associated grades are:

Grade	Room Use
A	Aseptic preparation and filling (critical zones under unidirectional flow)
B	A room containing a Grade A zone (the background environment for filling) and the area demarcated as the 'Aseptic Filling Suite' (including final stage changing rooms)
C	Preparation of solutions to be filtered and production processing; component handling.
D	Handling of components after washing; plasma stripping
U*	Freezers, computer conduits, store rooms, electrical cupboards, other rooms not in use etc.

* U = unclassified. Unclassified areas are not monitored.

Thus Grade A is the highest grade (that is the 'cleanest') and Grade D the lowest (that is the least 'clean'). ISO 14644 equivalents are detailed below.

CLASS	Number of Particles per Cubic Metre by Micrometre Size					
	0.1 um	0.2 um	0.3 um	0.5 um	1 um	5 um
ISO 1	10	2				
ISO 2	100	24	10	4		
ISO 3	1,000	237	102	35	8	
ISO 4	10,000	2,370	1,020	352	83	
ISO 5	100,000	23,700	10,200	3,520	832	29
ISO 6	1,000,000	237,000	102,000	35,200	8,320	293
ISO 7				352,000	83,200	2,930
ISO 8				3,520,000	832,000	29,300
ISO 9				35,200,000	8,320,000	293,000

ISO 14644-1 count levels

Another type of cleanzone is an Isolator. Isolators are superior to cleanrooms in that the contamination risk is reduced through the construction of a barrier between the critical area (sometimes called the 'micro-environment') and the outside environment. Isolators are used for sterility testing, aseptic filing and other applications where a clean environment is required. It is important that any possibility of contamination is avoided so that a 'false positive' does not occur.

What are clean air devices?

Within cleanrooms are various clean air devices. The terminology of ISO 14644-7, Cleanrooms and associate controlled environments - Part 7, uses the term 'Separative Devices' to collectively describe clean air hoods, gloveboxes, isolators and minienvironments. These devices include laminar airflows (more commonly described as Uni-Directional Airflow (UDAF) Devices in the context of pharmaceutical manufacturing given that 'true' laminarity cannot be easily demonstrated), Biosafety Cabinets and Isolators. Such devices normally operate at EU GMP Grade A / ISO Class 5. The term 'cabinet' is used more widely within Europe and the term 'hood' used more widely in the USA.

Whereas most cleanrooms operate with a turbulent airflow, clean air devices are designed to minimize turbulence which creates dust and dirt collection pockets by operating with the air blowing in one direction (uni-direcitonal), where the design feature is to move air away from the critical activity to ensure that any contamination is blown away to a less critical area.

With UDAF devices these are either constructed with horizontal flow or vertical flow. Specially designed UDAFs are biosafety cabinets. These are 'self-contained' enclosures which provide protection for personnel, environment and/ or products in work with hazardous microorganisms. The cabinets provide protection by creating an air barrier at the work opening and by HEPA filtration of exhaust air. Class I cabinets protect the operation or the product from personnel contamination, whereas Class II cabinets protect personnel, environment and products.

For some UDAF devices, gloves are fitted in order to restrict the number of personnel interventions. Such devices are described as Restrict Access Barrier Systems (RABS). These stand partway between a conventional UDAF and an isolator.

Another special type of cabinet is the powder containment cabinet. These are compact containment cabinets with inward airflow and HEPA filtration that provide protection for operators and the environment from powders generated by processes such as compounding of pharmaceuticals.

Another type of clean air device is an Isolator. Isolators are superior to cleanrooms in that the contamination risk is reduced through the construction of a barrier between the critical area (sometimes called the 'micro-environment') and the outside environment. Isolators are used for sterility testing, aseptic filing and other applications where a clean environment is required. It is important that any possibility of contamination is avoided so that a 'false positive' does not occur.

A variation of an isolator is a glovebox. A glovebox is an enclosure, fitted with sealed gloves, that allows external manual manipulations in controlled or hazardous environments.

What are pass-through or transfer hatches?

Many cleanrooms contain pass-through hatches. These are hatches with double doors that protect critical environments while allowing transfer or materials to or from adjoining rooms. They are typically installed within the walls of cleanrooms. The hatches allow materials to be transferred with minimal loss of room pressure and without the need for personnel movement between rooms.

What are airlocks?

An airlock is an airtight room which adjoins two cleanrooms. The airlock acts as a buffer zone between two independent areas of unequal pressure. A pressure differential of ≥ 15 Pa is typically maintained between the inner room and the air lock; and between the air lock and the external area (see later for information relating to pressure differentials).

What is contamination?

Cleanrooms are designed to minimise and to control contamination. There are many sources of contamination. The atmosphere contains dust, microorganisms, condensates, and gases. Manufacturing processes will also produce a range of contaminants. Wherever there is a process which grinds, corrodes, fumes, heats, sprays, turns, etc., particles and fumes are emitted and will contaminate the surroundings.

People, in clean environments, are the greatest contributors to contamination emitting body vapours, dead skin, micro-organisms, skin oils, and so on. The average person sheds 1,000,000,000 skin cells per day, of which 10% have micro-organisms on them. This demonstrates the importance of wearing cleanroom clothing and wearing this clothing correctly.

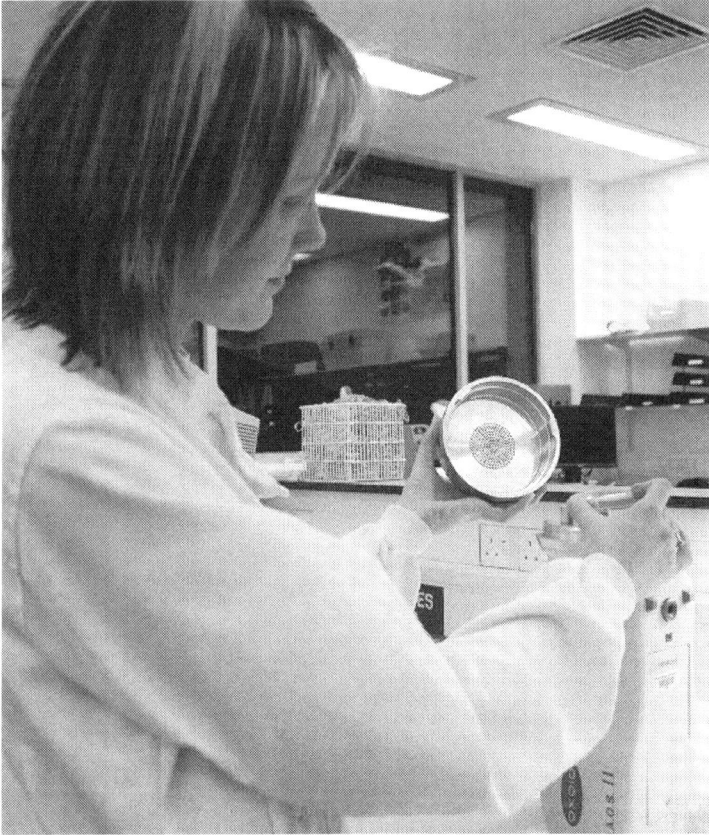

Photograph: Operator preparing an active air sampler for environmental monitoring

Most cleanroom micro-organisms are in the air. If they settle on a dry surface they are unlikely to survive and ideally any contamination is removed from the room. The biggest concern is water, which is both a vector and a growth source for micro-organisms.

Second to people, the key contamination source is water. This is an important issue for water is the main ingredient in many products, and it is used widely throughout the main process areas.

What is contamination control?

Contamination control is critical to all aspects of pharmaceutical manufacturing. Practices are put in place to ensure that the air is of the correct standard; that opportunities for contamination are not present (like water puddles on the floor); and that contamination carried on people is minimised.

Other ways by which contamination is controlled are:

- The air entering a cleanroom from outside is filtered to exclude dust, and the air inside is constantly re-circulated through HEPA filters. This is controlled through a HVAC (Heating, Ventilation and Air Conditioning) system. The most important part of this is with air-filtration through a HEPA (High Efficiency Particulate Air) filters.
- Staff enter and leave through airlocks and wear protective clothing such as hats, face masks, gloves, boots and cover-alls.
- Equipment inside the cleanroom is designed to generate minimal air contamination. There are even specialised mops and buckets. Cleanroom furniture is also designed to produce a low amount of particles and to be easy to clean.
- Common materials such as paper, pencils, and fabrics made from natural fibres are excluded from the Aseptic Filling Suite.
- Some cleanrooms are kept at a higher air pressure so that if there are any leaks, air leaks out of the chamber instead of unfiltered air coming in.
- Cleanroom HVAC systems also control the humidity to low levels, such that extra precautions are necessary to prevent electrostatic discharges.

Contamination control also requires personnel to practice aseptic techniques; wear specially designed clothing; to clean the areas to the correct standard; and to behave in ways which will minimise contamination.

Why monitor air quality in cleanrooms?

Air is both a means to ensure that cleanrooms are clean and it can be a source of contamination. Air cannot be avoided for without air we cannot breathe so as long as we require personnel to operate our processes we need an air supply.

Even in clean rural areas air is contaminated with about 108 particles of 0.5µm and greater per m^3, many of these will be microorganisms depending on the nature of the area and the season of the year: so air is a contamination problem. However in the pharmaceutical industry air flow is the answer to many contamination problems (as discussed in relation to the physical monitoring of cleanrooms below).

In order to ensure that cleanrooms are operating correctly, air is monitored through:

- Formal classification of cleanrooms (as defined by air cleanliness, which relates to the number of airborne particles)
- Through physical measurements of HVAC operations
- Through non-viable particle monitoring
- Through viable particle monitoring

There are four principles applying to control of air-borne microorganisms in clean rooms.

- Filtration (through the use of HEPA filters)

- Dilution (to ensure that particles generated in clean rooms, in addition to those which pass the filters, are carried away by diluting the clean area with new "clean" air)
- Directional Air Flow (to ensure that air blows away from critical zones, as particles and microorganisms cannot "swim upstream" against a directional air flow)
- Air Movement (rapid air movement is important for as long as particles and microorganisms stay suspended in the air they are not really a problem, for it is only when they settle out that they become an actual cause of contamination)

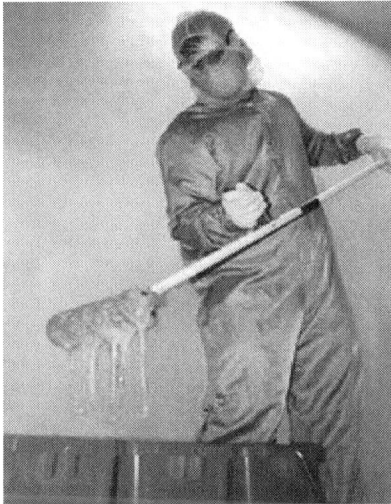

Photograph: An operator cleaning within a cleanroom

Different operating conditions

Clean rooms have three different 'states' of use. These are:

- As built;
- Static;
- Dynamic.

As built refers to the condition of a newly built clean room, with the operational qualification having been completed, at the point it is handed over to the user for performance qualification.

For static conditions is the room without personnel present, following 15 – 20 minutes 'clean up time', but with equipment operating normally.

Dynamic conditions (or 'operational') are defined as rooms being used for normal processing activities with personnel present and equipment operating.

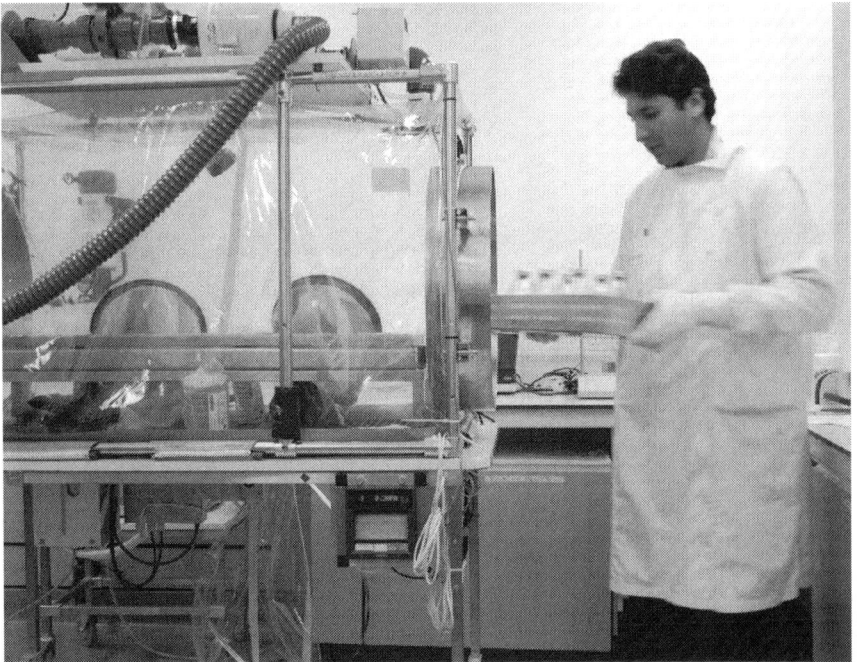

Photograph: A technician preparing an isolator for testing

Part B: Cleanroom classification

In order to ensure that cleanrooms and their HVAC systems are functioning correctly, they are classified at different intervals (Grade A and B six-monthly, and other cleanrooms annually). Classification of cleanrooms is confirmed in the dynamic state by taking non-viable particulate readings at a defined number of locations for 5.0μm and 0.5μm size particles.

Once a room has been assigned a classification, certain environmental parameters (physical and microbiological) are to be met on a routine basis. For viable monitoring it is normal for the microbiologist to set action levels based on an historical analysis of data.

The frequency of the assessment of these other parameters should be assessed based on a risk management approach. This approach should consider the room use and the risk to the product. Factors to consider may include room activities; exposure risk; room temperature; process stage; duration of process activities; water exposure and so on.

The recommended emphasis is upon environmental control rather than simply environmental monitoring.

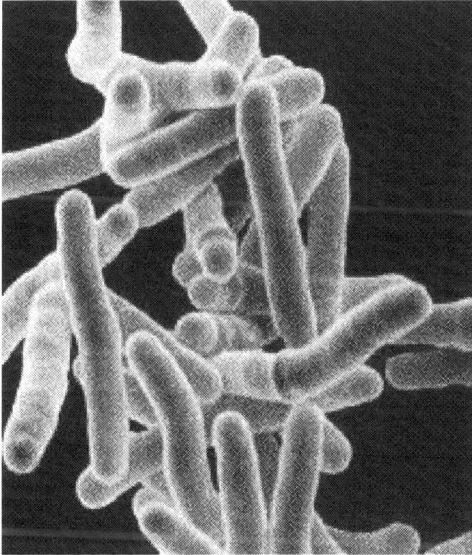

Photograph: Electron micrograph of a Bacillus spp. (bacteria), representative of cleanroom contamination.

HVAC operation

There are a number of physical parameters which require examination on a regular basis. These parameters generally relate to the operation of HVAC systems and the associated air-handling units. Air handler, or air handling unit (AHU) relates to the blower, heating and cooling elements, filter racks or chamber, dampers, humidifier, and other central equipment in direct contact with the airflow.

The key areas of HVAC operation essential for contamination control are:

Air-patterns and air-movement

Airflows, for critical activities, need to be studied in order to show that air turbulence does not interfere with critical processes by mapping smoke patterns. There are two types of cleanroom: turbulent flow or uni-directional flow, depending upon the required application. Uni-directional airflow areas are used for higher cleanliness states (such as aseptic filling) and they use far greater quantities of air than turbulent flow areas.

Airflows

Grade A zones (undirectional airflow devices in Grade B rooms) have a requirement for controlled air velocity and unidirectional air flow (either horizontal or vertical). These are monitored using an anemometer. The air velocity is designed to be sufficient to remove any relatively large particles before they settle onto surfaces.

Air changes

Each clean room grade has a set number of air changes per hour. A typical air conditioned office will have something between two and ten air changes per hour in order to give a level of comfort. The number of required air changes in a cleanroom is typically much higher. Air changes are provided in order to dilute any particles present to an acceptable concentration (thus air change is a way of expressing the level of air dilution which is occurring).

Clean up times

Connected to air changes is the time taken for a clean area to return to the static condition, appropriate to its grade, in terms of particulates.

Positive Pressure

Connected to the measurement of air flow is positive pressure. In order to maintain air quality in a clean room the pressure of a given room must be greater relative to a room of a lower grade. This is to ensure that air does not pass from " dirtier" adjacent areas into the higher grade clean room (this can also be observed by smoke studies). Generally this is 15-20 Pascals, although some areas of the same grade will also have differential pressure requirements due to specific activities. The most commonly encountered problems relate to situations when cleanroom doors are opened and here it can be difficult to maintain pressures.

HEPA filters

HEPA (High Efficiency Particulate Air) filters are used in to provide clean air to the cleanroom. HEPA filters are replaceable, extended-media, dry-type filters in rigid frames with set particle collection efficiencies. The filters are designed to control the number of particles entering a clean area by filtration. In Grade A zones HEPA filters also function to straighten the airflow as part of the unidirectional flow. In order to measure the effectiveness of the filters they are checked for leaks. Leakage is assessed by challenging the filters with a particle generating substance and measuring the efficiency of the filter.

HEPA filters function through a combination of three important aspects. First, there are one or more outer filters that work like sieves to stop the larger particles of dirt, dust, and hair. Inside those filters, there is a concertina - a mat of very dense fibres - which traps smaller particles. The inner part of the HEPA filter uses three different mechanisms to catch particles as they pass through in the moving airstream. At high air speeds, some particles are caught and trapped as they smash directly into the fibres, while others are caught by the fibres as the air moves past. At lower air speeds, particles tend to wander about more randomly through the filter (via Brownian motion) and may stick to the fibres as they do so. Together, these three mechanisms allow HEPA filters to catch particles that are both larger and smaller than a certain target size.

There are different grades of HEPA filters based on their 'efficiency ratings'. One of the most commonly used HEPA filter is the H14 filter, which is designed to remove 99.997% of particles from the air. HEPA Filters are protected from blockage by pre-filters which remove up to about 90% of particles from air.

To use an example, if air contains about 3×10^8 particles per m^3, and there is one pre-filter and one HEPA Filter:

- Pre-filter leaves about 3×10^7 per m^3 as a challenge to the HEPA filter

- The terminal HEPA Filter leaves about 10^3 per m^3.

- In EU GMP this is within the limits for Grade A and B "at rest" (Annex 1.4)

In Grade A zones HEPA filters also function to straighten the airflow as part of the unidirectional flow. In order to measure the effectiveness of the filters they are checked for leaks. Leakage is assessed by challenging the filters with a particle generating substance and measuring the efficiency of the filter.

Other factors

For certain cleanrooms temperature, humidity and lighting require control, either because of a process step or as a means to minimise contamination.

Photograph: Operator working within a cleanroom

Part C: Contamination Control

Contamination

Cleanrooms are designed to minimise and to control contamination. There are many sources of contamination. The atmosphere contains dust, microorganisms, condensates, and gases. Manufacturing processes will also produce a range of contaminants. Wherever there is a process which grinds, corrodes, fumes, heats, sprays, turns, etc., particles and fumes are emitted and will contaminate the surroundings.

People, in clean environments, are the greatest contributors to contamination emitting body vapours, dead skin, micro-organisms, skin oils, and so on. The average person sheds 1,000,000,000 skin cells per day, of which 10% have micro-organisms on them. This demonstrates the importance of wearing cleanroom clothing and wearing this clothing correctly.

Most cleanroom micro-organisms are in the air. If they settle on a dry surface they are unlikely to survive and ideally any contamination is removed from the room. The biggest concern is water, which is both a vector and a growth source for micro-organisms.

Second to people, the key contamination source is water. This is an important issue for water is the main ingredient in many products, and it is used widely throughout the main process areas.

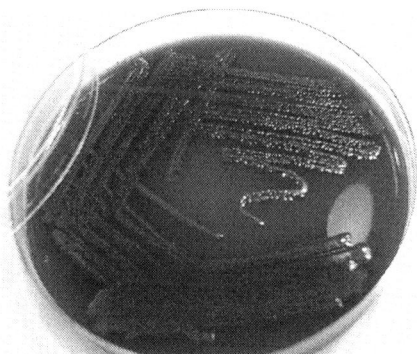

Photograph: microbiological agar plate for the isolation of a contaminant back in the microbiology laboratory.

Contamination control

Contamination control is critical to all aspects of pharmaceutical manufacturing. Practices are put in place to ensure that the air is of the correct standard; that opportunities for contamination are not present (like water puddles on the floor); and that contamination carried on people is minimised.

Other ways by which contamination is controlled are:

- The air entering a cleanroom from outside is filtered to exclude dust, and the air inside is constantly re-circulated through HEPA filters. This is controlled through a HVAC (Heating, Ventilation and Air Conditioning) system. The most important part of this is with air-filtration through a HEPA (High Efficiency Particulate Air) filters.
- Staff enter and leave through airlocks and wear protective clothing such as hats, face masks, gloves, boots and cover-alls.
- Equipment inside the cleanroom is designed to generate minimal air contamination. There are even specialised mops and buckets. Cleanroom furniture is also designed to produce a low amount of particles and to be easy to clean.
- Common materials such as paper, pencils, and fabrics made from natural fibres are excluded from the Aseptic Filling Suite.
- Some cleanrooms are kept at a higher air pressure so that if there are any leaks, air leaks out of the chamber instead of unfiltered air coming in.
- Cleanroom HVAC systems also control the humidity to low levels, such that extra precautions are necessary to prevent electrostatic discharges.

Contamination control also requires personnel to practice aseptic techniques; wear specially designed clothing; to clean the areas to the correct standard; and to behave in ways which will minimise contamination.

Contamination incidents

There are several types of contamination incident that can occur within cleanrooms. These tend to occur because:

a) Water is left on floors, which allows micro-organisms to grow;
b) Equipment is used wet;
c) Equipment which is clean has not been properly segregated from equipment which is wet;
d) Cleaning and disinfection is not undertaken to defined frequencies;
e) Air-lock doors do not open or close properly, allowing contaminated area to move between areas;
f) Personnel are not dressed correctly and allow contamination to spread.

Environmental monitoring

Environmental monitoring is a programme which examines the numbers and occurrences of viable micro-organisms and 'non-viable' particles (that is particles in the area other than micro-organisms like dust or skin cells). Ideally, environmental monitoring is targeted to those areas of the production process where the risk cannot be adequately controlled. It thereby, through trend analysis, provides an indication if the cleanroom is moving out-of-control.

Non-viable monitoring is for air-borne particle counts. These are the same sizes of particles required for the classification: 0.5 and 5.0 μm. This is undertaken using an optical particle counter. Particle counters are used to determine the air quality by counting and sizing the number of particles in the air.

What are particles?

'Particle' in the context of a cleanroom is a general term for subvisible matter. Airborne Particles, refers to particles suspended in air. Air contains a variety of different particles of a range of different sizes. These are particles of dust, dirt, skin, microorganisms and so on. As discussed above, the function of cleanrooms is to reduce the number of airborne particles (for example, an office building air contains from 500,000 to 1,000,000 particles (0.5 microns or larger) per cubic foot of air. In contrast, an ISO Class 5 / EU GMP Grade A cleanroom is designed not to allow more than 100 particles (0.5 microns or larger) per cubic foot of air.

With cleanrooms the regulatory standards, which are discussed below, focus on two sizes of particles which are selected due to the potential risk that they pose. These are:

- 0.5μm size particles, which are close in size to many microorganisms;
- 5.0 μm size particles, which are close in size to skin flakes, on which many microorganisms are bound to.

With European GMP, there is concern with both types of particle size. With the FDA, the primary focus is upon the 0.5μm size.

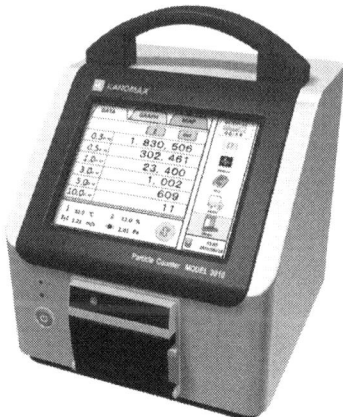

Photograph: Particle counter

What is the unit of measurement for particles?

The unit of measurement for particles is the micrometer (or 'micron'). This is symbolised as μm. The micron is a unit of length equal to one millionth (10^{-6}) of a metre.

What are the Sources of Particles in Cleanrooms?

Particles are generated from a variety of sources. These can include:

- Facilities, such as: walls, floors and ceilings; paint and coatings; construction material; air conditioning debris; room air and vapours; spills and leaks.
- People, including: skin flakes and oil; cosmetics and perfume; spittle; clothing debris (lint, fibres etc.); hair.
- Equipment generated, including: friction and wear particles, lubricants and emissions, vibrations
- Cleaning equipment, like: brooms, mops and dusters; cleaning chemicals
- Fluids, arising from spillages
- Particulates floating in air, primarily: bacteria, fungi, organic material and moisture
- Compressed gasses
- Product generated

Within cleanrooms the primary concern is with those particles which are microorganisms or likely to be carrying microorganisms, such as skin flakes. The major source, and hence the primary risk, is from people. The risk can be increased through physical behaviour like fast motion and horseplay or from physiological concerns like room temperature, humidity or from psychological concerns like claustrophobia, odours and workplace attitude. In general, people produce contamination via:

- Body Regenerative Processes: skin flakes, oils, perspiration and hair.
- Behaviour: rate of movement, sneezing and coughing.
- Attitude: work habits and communication between personnel.

A degree of protection is provided through cleanroom clothing. Cleanroom gowns are manufactured from special materials which are designed to minimise the amount of contamination which can be shed from the skin, provided that the gown is not worn of an excessive time and that the temperature is not too high. Special apparel includes non-shedding gowns or coveralls, head covers, face masks, gloves, footwear or shoe covers.

What are particle counters?

Particle counting is performed using a variety of optical particle counters (aerosols passed through a focused light source, where the scattered light is converted into electrical pulses which allow the counting of particles). These are designed to detect the number of particles of a given size from a given volume of air. The types of counters used are detailed in Microbiology method SOPs. Some particle counters maybe connected to a Facility Monitoring System (FMS).

A particle counter is a device which draws air in using a pump at a controlled flow rate. The air is passed into a sensor area and through a light beam created by a laser diode. The amount of light reflected from each particle is measured electronically (as an electronic pulse). The larger the particle, then the larger the amount of reflected light (the greater the height of the light pulse). This allows the particle counter to 'count' the number of particles in a given volume of air (as the number of light pulses) and to assess the size of the particles counted.

Different particle counters have different **flow rates**. The flow rate is the rate at which air is drawn into a particle counter, and thus the time taken for the counter to measure a fixed volume of air. The long standing flow rate has been 1.0 cubic feet per minute (equivalent to 28.3 litres per minute). This flow rate is the baseline for cleanroom certification.

What is particle loss?

Particle loss is minimised by the use of specialised tubing (such as Bev-a-line or Tygon tubing) which is designed to prevent particles from adhering to the tubing surface. Thus the quality of the material used for particle counter tubing is important. In general, there are three types of tubing which may be considered:

a) Bev-A-Line tubing or Tygon tubing

Bev-A-Line or Tygon tubing tubing is a co-extruded tubing consisting of a PVC exterior and a Hytrel interior. Its suitability as a tubing for particle counters relates to the smoothness of the interior wall.

b) Stainless steel

Stainless steel tubing is suitable for situations where particles in a hot air-stream require measurement (such as a dehydrogenation tunnel). The disadvantage of the tubing is its lack of flexibility.

c) Polyurethane

Particle loss can also occur due to tubing diameter. The recommended internal diameter of tubing for particle counters, by particle counter manufacturers, is ¼". This may vary depending upon the flow rate of the counter (Pollen, a, p2). The tubing used at BPL has a diameter of 10-15mm (refer to approved purchase register). This ensures that the tubing has the correct Reynolds number.

Particle counter tubing lengths must be kept as short as possible. This is particularly important for avoiding particle loss for particles of a size of >1.0 micron. Research suggests that there is a 20% loss of 5.0 micron particle counts for tubing lengths of >3 metres (approximately 10 feet). Particle counter tubing should not exceed 3 metres in length between the sampling head probe and the particle counter. This is to ensure the transportation and delivery of larger particles (such as 5.0 µm) and to avoid 'drop-out'. Tubing should also be as straight as possible. Radial bends will result in the loss of particles (Pollen, a, p3)

Particle counters tubing must be changed at regular intervals (such as three-monthly). All particle counter tubing will, over time, accumulate particles, particularly where particle counters are used for continuous monitoring. A phenomenon which can arise is the sudden release of particles (previously suspended on tubing walls) which may lead to an unusually high count or series of counts.

What different counting modes do particle counters have?

Particle counters can be set for one of two counting modes:

i) **Cumulative count**: where the counter is set to count the number of particles for the selected size and greater. For example, if a counter is set to count 0.5 µm particles, it will count all particles at the 0.5 µm and greater (such as 0.5, 0.7, 1.0, 5.0 and 10.0, depending upon the number of available channels on the counter). For cleanroom classification and for particle monitoring for EU GMP, the cumulative mode must always be used.

ii) **Differential mode**: where the counter is set to only count the number of particles of the selected size. For example, if a counter is set to count 0.5 µm particles, it will only count particles of the 0.5 µm size.

What is microbiological environmental monitoring?

Environmental monitoring is a programme which examines the numbers and occurrences of viable micro-organisms (as wells as 'non-viable' particles as discussed above). Ideally, environmental monitoring is targeted to those areas of the production process where the risk cannot be adequately controlled. It thereby, through trend analysis, provides an indication if the cleanroom is moving out-of-control.

What is viable monitoring?

Viable monitoring is designed to detect levels of bacteria and fungi present in defined locations /areas during a particular stage in the activity of processing and filling a product. Samples are taken from walls, surfaces, people and the air (each of which represents a potential contamination source). Viable monitoring is designed to detect micro-organisms and answer the questions: how may?; how frequent?; when do they occur?; why do they occur?

Viable monitoring is undertaken using a substance called agar (a jelly-like growth medium) in different sized containers. Sometimes mechanical devices are used to pull in a defined quantity of air (an air-sampler).

The environmental monitoring programme is normally controlled by the Microbiology Department who establish the appropriate frequencies and durations for monitoring based on a risk assessment approach. The sampling plan takes into account the cleanliness level required at each site to be sampled.

What are the methods used for viable monitoring?

Viable microbiological monitoring is normally performed using the following methods:

Table:

Method	Air	Surface	Personnel
1	Active air Sampler (cfu/m³)	Contact Plate (cfu/25cm²)	Finger plate for Hands (cfu/5 fingers) Contact plate for gowns (cfu/25cm²)
2	Settle Plate (cfu/90mm over x time)[1]	Swab (cfu/surface)	

---

[1] Normally time is per four hours. With the exception of short duration events (such as filtration of product into the filling suite or filling machine set-up) results are expressed as cfu / 4 hours. Where exposure is less than 4 hours ('routine' monitoring uses a time of not less than one hour) results are extrapolated to cfu / 4 hours. For the exceptions mentioned, results are reported as cfu / event. The reason for using cfu / event is that where activities are less than 30 minutes duration there remains a danger that a degree of distortion would occur which would lead to a result which was not commensurate with the risk.

Where cfu = Colony Forming Unit

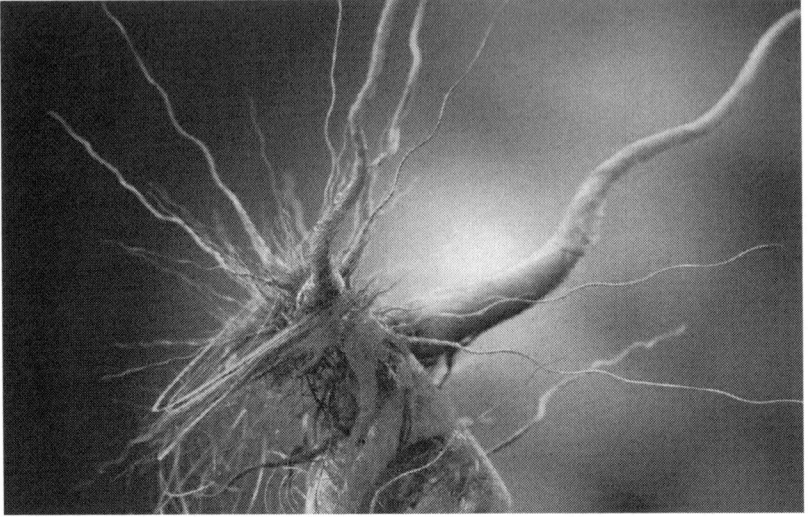

Photograph: representative image of a bacterium

Part D: Critical Cleanroom Parameters

Cleanroom classification

The two main ways by which cleanrooms are classified. This is either to EU GMP or to ISO 14644. There are differences between the two standards whether cleanrooms are operating in the static or dynamic states.

When referring to room grades, the following are equivalent under **static** conditions:

EU GMP	ISO 14644-1
A	4.8
B	5
C	7
D	8

When referring to room grades, the following are equivalent under **dynamic** conditions:

EU GMP	ISO 14644-1
A	4.8
B	7
C	8
D	9

Clean rooms can be classified in one of three occupancy states, as built, static or dynamic. It is more typical for clean rooms to be classified in the **dynamic** state (or 'operational') by taking non-viable particulate readings at a defined number of locations for $5.0\mu m$ and $0.5\mu m$ size particulates (as defined in a sampling plan) at the following approximate frequencies (as stated in ISO 14644-2):

Grade	Frequency of classification
A	Six-monthly
B	Six-monthly
C	Annually
D	Annually

The **method** for classification is detailed in SOP QBS/00181, which has been **based on** ISO 14644-1. There is a slight difference in the limits between EU GMP and ISO 14644. In this case, EU GMP limits have been taken. This is detailed in rationale LR1156.

The sampling locations for the classification of a clean room is derived from the formula in ISO 14644-1. Establishment of the sampling locations is based on the area of the room.

The formula is:

$$N_L = \sqrt{A}$$

Where:

N_L is the minimum number of sampling locations (rounded up to a whole number).

A is the area of the clean room or clean zone in square metres (m^2) for which the square root is taken.

Sampling is based on the 0.5 μm particle size. Once the number of samples has been calculated, samples are to be taken at approximately equal distance apart (by dividing the clean area into a grid whilst taking into account fixed equipment). Samples are to be taken approximately one metre from the floor or at the height of the work activity. Only one sample is required to be taken from each location unless there is only one location in the clean area, in this case three samples are required. A sample is a minimum of 20 counts/readings for a minimum sample volume of 2 litres. A 95% UCL is applied when there is ≤9 sample locations in a clean area.

At each sample location a sufficient volume of air should be sampled so that a minimum of 20 particles would be detected if the particle concentration of the 5.0μm size was the class limit for the designated class.

Photograph: HEPA filter

Particle count limits

The following limits are the maximum levels allowed in a clean room, as per EU GMP Guide.

Parameters	Grade A		Grade B		Grade C		Grade D	
Non-viable	Particle size/m³		Particle size/m³		Particle size/m³		Particle size/m³	
particulates Static State	3, 520 at 0.5μm	20 at 5.0μm	3, 520 at 0.5μm	29 at 5.0μm	352,000 at 0.5μm	2,900 at 5.0μm	3,520,000 at 0.5μm	29,000 at 5.0μm
Non-viable	Particle size/m³		Particle size/m³		Particle size/m³		Particle size/m³	
particulates Dynamic State	3, 520 at 0.5μm	20 at 5.0μm	352,000 at 0.5μm	2,900 at 5.0μm	3, 520,000 at 0.5μm	29,000 at 5.0μm	Not defined*	Not defined*

C/m³ = count per cubic metre

Airflows

Airflows, for critical activities in relation to aseptic filling, need to be studied in order to show that air turbulence does not interfere with critical processes. All critical rooms and zones within the Aseptic Filling area relating to batch filling will be assessed by Microbiology. Other critical processes may also be monitored.

Specification	Source of specification	Frequency	Method
Visual assessment of risk to process	None – although recommended practice.	To be determined by the user.	Smoke generation and mapping

Note: For air flow movement, air flow must be from a higher grade area to a lower grade area.

Air velocity

Grade A zones (undirectional airflow devices in Grade B rooms) have a requirement for controlled air velocity and unidirectional air flow (either horizontal or vertical). These are monitored using an anemometer. The air velocity is designed to be sufficient to remove any relatively large particles before they settle onto surfaces.

This monitoring is performed routinely and during re-qualification exercises.

Specification	Source of specification	Frequency	Method
0.45 m/s +/- 20% (unidirectional)	EU GMP	Six monthly	Anemometer

The FDA Guide to Aseptic Filling does not specify an air velocity but requires one to be justified. The specification used is taken from the EU GMP Guide. The specification has been proved effective based on airflow (smoke) study investigations, which have demonstrated that this air speed is of sufficient velocity to remove contamination from Grade A filling machines.

The FDA Guide requires airflow measurements to be taken at 6" from the filter face and "proximal to the work surface". The EU GMP Guide requires readings to be taken at the working height. Working height is defined in local procedures and demonstrated as effective by way of airflow (smoke) studies. The practice at many organisations, during bi-annual re-qualifications, is that airflows will be measured from both locations using the specification detailed in the table above.

In addition to qualifications, many organisations elect to measure airflows periodically before commencing an activity.

Air changes – general guidance

Each clean room grade has a set number of air changes per hour. Air changes are provided in order to dilute any particles present to an acceptable concentration. Any contamination produced in the clean room is theoretically removed within the required time appropriate to the room grade. Monitoring air changes is necessary because the re-circulation of filtered air is important for maintaining control of the clean area.

Air change rates stated are the minimum and should be calculated from supply air volume and room volume measurements. Previous standards have stipulated 20 air-changes per hour as the minimum. This remains a reasonable set minimum, although frequently more frequent air-changes are desirable.

Clean up times

Connected to air changes is the time taken for a clean area to return to the static condition, appropriate to its grade, in terms of particulates.

Specification	Source of specification	Method
All clean rooms 15 – 20 minutes to achieve static classification	EU GMP / ISO 14644	Particle counting

The conducting of clean-up times is an optional test to be considered at the time of room classification; following substantial changes to room design; for newly built clean rooms or as part of an investigation.

According to EU GMP Guide (1st March 2009 revision) these 'clean-up' times apply to Grade A and B areas only. They may, however, be used as a guidance for Grade C and D areas in the course of an investigation.

Positive Pressure

Connected to the measurement of air flow is positive pressure. In order to maintain air quality in a clean room the pressure of a given room must be greater relative to a room of a lower grade. This is to ensure that air does not pass from "dirtier" adjacent areas into the higher grade clean room. Generally this is 15-20 Pascals, although some areas of the same grade at BPL also have differential pressure requirements due to specific activities.

Specification	Source of specification	Frequency	Method
15-20 Pa relative to lower grade rooms (for A this is relative to B; for A and B this is relative to C; for C this is relative to D)	EU GMP	Monitored every 20 seconds for Grade B rooms; monitored by Production staff for C and D areas	Electronic micro-manometer

Note: Pressure differentials (expressed in Pascals) are the relative pressures from a higher grade area into a lower one. These are guidance values taken from EU GMP Annex 1. There will be some exceptions to the criteria stated above for particular areas which require different pressure differentials.

HEPA filters

HEPA (High Efficiency Particulate Air) filters are designed to control the number of particles entering a clean area by filtration. In Grade A zones HEPA filters also function to straighten the airflow as part of the unidirectional flow. In order to measure the effectiveness of the filters they are checked for leaks. Leakage is assessed by challenging the filters with a particle generating substance and measuring the efficiency of the filter.

Specification	Source of specification	Frequency	Method
99.997% (minimum efficiency)	BS EN 1822	Six monthly	Smoke generator / photometer

Note: HEPA filter integrity taken from BS EN 1822 Parts 1 and 2. The 99.997% efficiency is based on particle sizes 0.3 μm and larger (i.e. theoretically only 3 out of 10,000 particles at 0.3μm size can penetrate the filter).

Temperature, humidity, lighting and room design

Grade B rooms have set requirements for temperature and humidity. These are monitored for operator comfort and to avoid a high temperature – humidity situation which may result in the shedding of micro-organisms. Other clean areas have a temperature appropriate to the process step (e.g. if the process requires a cold room at 2-8°C).

Lighting should be adequate, uniform and anti-glare, to allow operators to perform process tasks effectively. A range of 400 to 750 lux is recommended.

Specification	Source of specification	Frequency	Method
Grade B Temperature: $18 \pm 3°C$	BPL Site Master File	Monitored by production staff	Thermometer
Humidity: $45 \pm 15\%$	ISO14644-4		Humidity reader

Clean rooms are specially designed rooms. The surfaces are constructed from materials that do not generate particles, and are easy to clean.

References

A) Regulatory

- EU GMP Guide Annexe 1
- USP #26 <1116>
- FDA Guide to Aseptic Processing 2004: 'Guidance for Industry – Sterile Drug Products Produced by Aseptic Processing – Current Good Manufacturing Practice', Revised September 2004
- ISO 14644-1: 'Cleanrooms and associated controlled environments, Part 1: Classification of air cleanliness'
- ISO 14644-2: Specification for testing cleanrooms to prove continued compliance with ISO 14644-1

B) Other

- Akey, J. (2005): 'Info Overload: What Do My Particle Counts Mean?', *Indoor Environment Connections*, Volume 6, Issue 11
- Akey, J. 'Validation, Calibration Assure Investigation Accuracy', *Lighthouse*, USA
- Halls, N. (2004): 'Effects and causes of contamination in sterile manufacturing' in Hall, N. (ed.): 'Microbiological Contamination Control in Pharmaceutical Clean Rooms', CRC Press, Boca Raton, pp1-22
- Johnson, S. M. (2004): 'Microbiological Environmental Monitoring' in Hodges, N. and Hanlon, G. 'Microbiological Standards and Controls', Euromed, London
- Lovegrove-Saville, P. and Perry, M. (2000): 'Setting environmental alert and action limits', PharMIG News, Issue 3, December 2000
- PDA Technical Report No. 13 (Revised): 'Fundamentals of an Environmental Monitoring Program', September – October 1997 (revised 2001)
- Pollen, M. (a) 'Particle Sample Tube Lengths for Pharmaceutical Monitoring', *Lighthouse*, USA
- Pollen, M. (b) 'Airborne Particle Counting for Pharmaceutical Facilities: Update 2008, EU GMP Annex 1', *Lighthouse*, USA
- Sandle, T. (2004): 'General Considerations for the Risk Assessment of Isolators used for Aseptic Processes', Pharmaceutical Manufacturing and Packaging Sourcer, Samedan Ltd, Winter 2004, pp43-47
- Vincent, D.(2002): 'Validating, Establishing and Maintaining A Routine Environmental Monitoring Program for Cleanroom Environments: Part 1', Journal of Validation Technology, August 2002, Vol. 8, No.4
- Whyte, W. (2001): 'Cleanroom Technology: Fundamentals of Design, Tetsing and Operation', Wiley
- Whyte, W. (ed.) (1999): 'Cleanroom Design', 2nd Edition, Wiley.
- Wilson, J. (1997): 'Setting alert / action limits for environmental monitoring programs', PDA Journal, Vol.51, No.4, July –August 1997

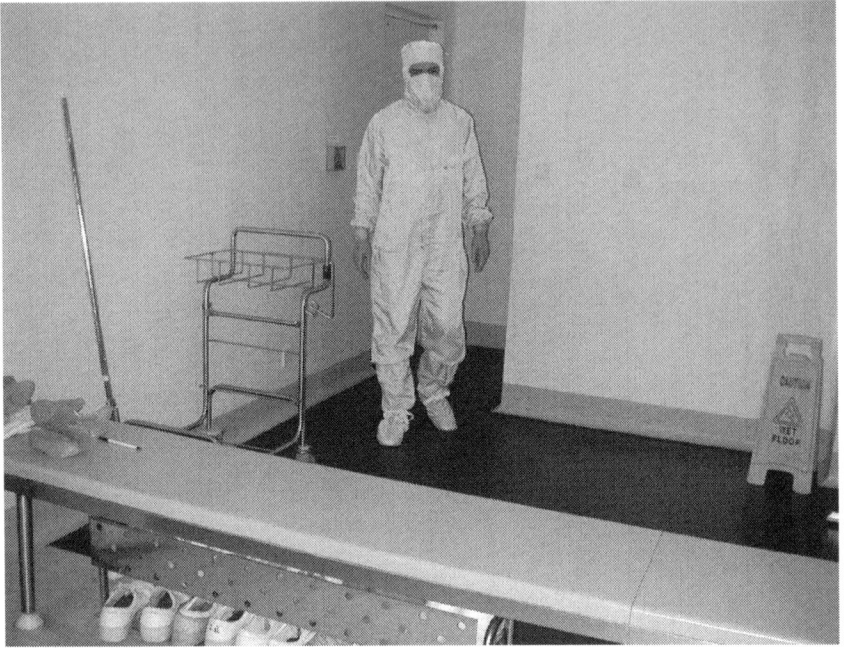

Made in the USA
Monee, IL
28 March 2026